Platform
Papers

Quarterly essays on the Performing Arts   No. 3: January 2005

CURRENCY HOUSE

PLATFORM PAPERS
Quarterly essays on the Performing Arts.
Editor: Dr John Golder, j.golder@unsw.edu.au

Currency House Inc. is a non-profit association and resource centre advocating the role of the performing arts in public life by research, debate and publication.
Postal address: PO Box 2270, Strawberry Hills, NSW 2012, Australia
Email: info@currencyhouse.org.au   Tel: (02) 9319 4953
Website: www.currencyhouse.org.au   Fax: (02) 9319 3649
Executive Officer: Eamon Flack
Editorial Board: Katharine Brisbane AM, Dr John Golder, John McCallum, Greig Tillotson

ISBN   0 9581213 7 0
ISSN   1449-583X

National Library of Australia Cataloguing-in-publication Data
Meyrick, Julian.
    Trapped by the past: why our theatre is facing paralysis.
    ISBN 0 9581213 7 0.
    1. Theater – Australia. I. Currency House Inc. II. Title. (Series: Platform papers; no. 3).
    700.0994

Cover design by Kate Florance
Typeset in 10.5 Arrus BT
Printed by Hyde Park Press, Adelaide

THE UNIVERSITY OF
NEW SOUTH WALES

Lawyers

The publication of *Platform Papers* is assisted by the University of New South Wales, Holman Webb Lawyers (Australia) and Gleebooks.

Contents

1   **TRAPPED BY THE PAST**
Why our theatre is facing paralysis
Julian Meyrick

70   **Readers' Forum**
Benjamin Marks and Clem Gorman on
Survival of the Fittest

AVAILABILITY   *Platform Papers*, quarterly essays on the performing arts, is published every January, April, July and October and is available through bookshops or by subscription (for order form, see page 86).

LETTERS   Currency House invites readers to submit letters of 400–1,000 words in response to the essays. Letters should be emailed to the Editor at j.golder@unsw.edu.au or posted to Currency House at PO Box 2270, Strawberry Hills, NSW 2012, Australia. To be considered for the next issue, the letters must be received by 8 February 2005.

CURRENCY HOUSE   For membership details, see our website at: www.currencyhouse.org.au

Trapped by the Past

Why our theatre is facing paralysis

JULIAN MEYRICK

The author

Julian Meyrick is Associate Director and Literary Adviser at the Melbourne Theatre Company and Hon. Associate in the Drama Program, La Trobe University. He has staged numerous productions in Sydney and Melbourne, including the notable *Who's Afraid of the Working Class?* and for the MTC Joe Penhall's *Blue/Orange*, Bryony Lavery's *Frozen* and Moira Buffini's *Dinner*. He has worked with writers such as Andrew Bovell, Patricia Cornelius, Christos Tsiolkas, Melissa Reeves, Catherine Zimdahl, Sam Sejavka, Jane Bodie and Ross Mueller. In 1998 he received a Green Room Award for Best Director on the Fringe. He has published on arts policy, performance theory/practice and post-war Australian theatre. His *See How It Runs: Nimrod and the New Wave* appeared in 2002.

Author's acknowledgements

I must acknowledge the support of the MTC and the La Trobe University Drama Program in the writing of this essay. I am especially grateful to Geoffrey Milne, Guy Rundle, Ann Tonks and Neil Pigot, who read early drafts and made valuable improvements; to Dale Bradbury for help with tables and charts; to John Baylis, Françoise Rodriguez and Jean MacDonald at the Australia Council, and Judy Seeff at the STC, for helping to locate key data, while Playbox Theatre courteously and courageously made available its recent attendance figures. Publisher Katharine Brisbane's intimate knowledge of Australian theatre history and John Golder's gimlet editorial eye have saved me from a number of errors. Finally, I especially thank the members of the small consortium that was, briefly, the Melbourne Independent Theatre Project—a good idea, whose time had not yet come.

Introduction

What is Australian theatre? The simplicity of the question belies the complexity of the answer, which varies according to who is asked. For theatre practitioners it is primarily an art form. For audiences a choice of stage productions. For critics a collation of aesthetic norms. For governments an area of social policy. For academics an object of scholarly attention. For donors an occasion for charity. For sponsors an opportunity for marketing. For administrators an endless procession of tight budgets and impossible standards. And so it goes on. To say that theatre, in Australia, is a creative activity that puts a particular artwork—a stage show— before a particular public is to say little about the myriad dimensions of its being. To get a handle on what Australian theatre is as an artistic, economic and institutional entity, we need to synthesise all such understandings and reflect on the results.

This is rarely done. Debate about theatre in Australia today means either arguments over resources and/or spats about personalities. The former involves the statistical analysis of generalised data, and is the preserve of governments and other official bodies. A surge in quantitative research in the cultural sector over the last twenty years has seen an avalanche of reporting on various computational aspects of theatre's existence. How theatre is housed, priced, sold, how it manages its revenue and cost streams—even, when the mood dictates, its artistic and cultural priorities—all these things have come under official scrutiny since the father of public inquiries into the performing arts, the much-maligned Guthrie Report, first showed governments how to do it in 1949. As for the personalities, praise and blame are heaped irregularly on individuals and organisations according to obscure, rapidly changing agendas. In a country where sport supplies the majority of life's master-metaphors, it is unsurprising that theatre should find itself wracked on the sterile binaries of an attenuated pseudo-athleticism. State theatres, international festivals, community theatres, fringe theatre and amateur theatre are taken up in a cause-ish way, treated like so many competing football teams. In the flurry of names and categories, practitioners conduct a deadly struggle for scarce resources with the gloves-off attitude of the not-so-quietly desperate.

Patronage and personalities: for a depressing number of people involved in theatre, and for many who wish it well, or tune in now and then for the latest developments, Australian theatre is a straightforward, if high-stakes, exercise in arithmetic. Take a bunch of money, give it to a bunch of artists and, hey presto, you've got theatre. All that remains is a war of attrition over secondary, related matters: how much money, through what means and to whom. And this war can be waged with weapons familiar since the art form's genesis as a state-supported industry in 1954—statistics and character assassination. From time to time, a form of theatre will find itself ensnared in the rhetorical crossfire, at which point it is quickly reduced to caricature (as New Wave drama found itself in the Whitlam years, or community theatre fifteen years later). But this happens less now than formerly. As a mark of general weediness, Australian theatre has succumbed to homogenisation and few outside the industry can tell apart its different strata, much less assign them specific cultural significance.

Such 'debates' about theatre do not tell us much about it. They do not tell us what intrinsically it is, or how it has developed. They do not say how we are to know when it is being done well or why it is worth doing at all. They do not fill us with hope for its future or knowledge of its extraordinary past—though theatre is an art form which is passionately historical and whose 2,500-year-old evolution is richly inscribed on its present shape. In short, they omit most of what we need to know about its purpose, value and methods of work, focusing instead on its social effects or on the vicissitudes of personal creativity. It's like trying to walk down the street with a telescope clapped to one eye and a microscope to the other. You can see everything except what you need to. If only we could leave aside these optical devices—useful after their fashion, but seriously compromised—and look with plainer sight. No government report or Sunday magazine article is going to help us here. To understand Australian theatre as a deep set of forces an entirely different approach is needed.

This essay attempts to provide just that. Like all points of view that seek to be broadly persuasive, it is part analysis, part adventure. The analysis is historical. Since I am a theatre historian and since the dimension missing from talk about Australian theatre is, above all, to do with its temporal development, then such an account is long overdue. The adventure is my own—the story of a theatre director, Anglo-Australian by birth, raised in one culture but discovering another, and still dealing with the fact. (If truth is the aim, then you cannot leave your own daily experience of the art form out, because, in the end, daily experience is all the art form is.) In approaching Australian theatre in such a bifurcated way, I hope to construct a mode of seeing it, both empathic and critical, which highlights key features of its emotional world. In a hermeneutic sense, I am less concerned with *explaining* Australian theatre than with *understanding* it, less interested in neat argument, partisanship and conceptual elaboration, than in ways of seeing and habits of mind. I want to pick my way through post-war Australian theatre, from an historical and a personal point of view, to promote a more sinewy and sincere understanding of its pathways.

Without this understanding there is no hope for a successful solution to the concatenation of problems the industry presents today. Right thinking produces right action. It is because the thinking about the art form is so feeble that many government initiatives in the sector are ineffective, belated, confused, pompous or self-serving; it is why so much arts journalism treats theatre as if it were an alien artefact dropped from outer space; why the art form finds so little purchase in the general consciousness of the Australian public, though it can easily follow the convoluted structures of the visual arts, literature and film. Like a drowning man in distant waters, Australian theatre struggles for life with all its might, while those not involved in its immediate fate perceive only a waving of arms and the occasional cry for help. This has got to change. Before anything else, the profession as a whole must embark on a heart-felt examination bent on answering one vital question: what on earth do we think we are doing? What do we imagine Australian theatre is, ontologically speaking, and what is the value in parcelling out portions of our life in support of it? Unless we have a grasp of our root involvement in the art form, then we are taking a living artistic medium and reducing it to a mentally inert production line of variable product whose purpose is mere self-perpetuation. We are doing more than wasting time, we are actively killing it.

Two over-riding concerns run through this essay, which are central to both what has happened to Australian theatre in the past, and how its burdens might be managed in the future:

1. That there is something meaningful called 'Australian theatre', and that it is a proper object of contemplation for anyone seriously interested in theatre in this country. In this respect both the idea and the reality of the concept have been at times badly mis-understood. Far from being coercively limiting and nationalistic, the bracketing notion 'Australian theatre' has historically acted as a mechanism of inclusion, pulling together widely disparate enterprises under a common umbrella of under-standing, empowering them both politically and culturally. The pursuit and perfection of 'Australian theatre' is a vital plank—*the* vital plank—in any living theatre culture. Ninety per cent of such national imaging may be unconscious and implicit—just the kind of theatre practitioners *do* without being self-consciously 'Australian' about it. The result is both welcome and necessary: forms of theatre that set out to explore experiences, real and imaginative, which pertain to the local communities bounded, economically, politically and geographically, by the nation-state known as 'Australia'.

2. That a series of disconnections has arisen within the body of efforts that constitutes the persona of Australian theatre whose chief fault-line is generational. Theatre companies, and the infrastructure underpinning them, are objects that persist through time. (The Melbourne Theatre Company (MTC) celebrated its fiftieth anniversary in 2003, and the other state companies are at least twenty-five years old.) How these institutions are penetrated by cohorts of differing ages who come looking for artistic employment is a matter which directly affects the health of the industry. Over-identification with one generation's sensibility can lead to disaster when audiences need to be replenished by attracting another—one reason why the Old Tote Theatre Company, predecessor to the Sydney Theatre Company (STC), went broke in 1978. But theatre cultures are more than collections of material assets. There are ideas, ways of working, attitudes and values which also need handing on, albeit in a transformed way, from older practitioners to younger ones. When this doesn't happen—or happens less often and meaningfully than it should—the result is stunted growth: a theatre culture which repeats itself, rather than growing richer, because it doesn't know how to manage its inheritance.

These two issues have profound implications for theatre in Australia. Both are being fuddled. The term 'Australian theatre' has reverted to being a flat description, and a faintly old-hat one at that. The notion—the *correct* notion—that the country is locked in a desperate struggle to define its own cultural identity in stage terms, does not have the currency it should. Rather, there has been, and for some time, an opposite assumption, that Australia succeeded in outlining the major contours of its theatrical persona at some definitive moment in time (the Whitlam years, say) and no further efforts, intellectually or practically, have been necessary. With the Free Trade Agreement breathing down our necks, it remains to be seen if this lazy and false attitude can survive unchallenged for much longer. But the fact that national imaging has been missing from official thinking about theatre for some time bodes ill for its future.

By contrast, the idea of generational change is on everyone's lips. A powerful idea—or one that would be, if it weren't so often treated in a superficial way. Generational change is almost physical agony for the theatre, whose most important assets are its body of skilled practitioners and hard-core subscriber audiences. From time to time, both modes of producing theatre and the sensibility underscoring the resulting work come under challenge, from within and outside the art form. At these moments, different ideas of what is good and bad, right and wrong, true and false grapple, sometimes very publicly, as new ways of working are developed. One of the most important recent battles remains the struggle for a self-consciously national drama of the 1970s—sometimes called New Wave theatre—to throw off what it perceived was an Anglo-obsessed legacy dating back to colonial times. Plays like David Williamson's *The Removalists*, Alex Buzo's *Norm and Ahmed*, John Romeril and Jack Hibberd's *Marvellous Melbourne*, Michael Boddy and Bob Ellis's *The Legend of King O'Malley*—as well as less text-based work by companies such as the Performance Syndicate and the Human Body Group—changed the face of Australian theatre forever. The ways in which it did so are complex. But the key to the shift is the idea of a 'generation', a new type of theatre being done by a new type of theatre practitioner. Where is the follow-on to that shift now? By rights, Australian theatre should be slap-bang in the middle of a newly emerging dramatic sensibility. Where is it? Is it not there to be found? Or is it there and yet not being supported as it should?

Talking about 'Australian theatre' in a general way is fraught with difficulty. For a start, there's its geographically dispersed nature. What currently passes for authoritative overview is often no more than an extrapolation from one kind of work in one city. 'The theatre' in the upper-middle-brow-makes-you-think-a-bit sense does not typically cover either the orgiastic populism of a *Lion King* or the local triumphs of the Rockhampton Players. In other words, 'the theatre' means government-supported, non-commercial, non-amateur theatre, usually in a state or territory capital. Depending on the critic's sympathies and habits, this is further reduced to the established companies (good thing/bad thing), or the fringe (living thing/dead thing) or periodic extravaganzas (festivals and the like). The results are remarks that don't resonate beyond the narrow range of experiences on which they are based.

There are two solutions to the problem: to buy a fistful of airfares and fly around the country seeing as many shows as possible; or to turn to history. As to the former, the number of people with genuine first-hand knowledge of theatre nationally can be counted on the fingers of one hand. Our only authentically national critic has been Katharine Brisbane, who wrote for the *Australian* between 1967 and 1974. The Sydney-based Australia Council discontinued its practice of regularly sending administrative officers interstate to view performances of its clients in the early 1990s. Currently, Australia doesn't even have a dedicated theatre magazine with national coverage.

However, the tyranny of distance can be alleviated by knowledge of the past. Though theatre practitioners and their press releases may bill their creative efforts as if they came from nowhere but their own unprecedented genius, no-one plays on our stages, from imposing arts centres to humble community halls, without the pattern of that work having been established deep in time. Why some artists operate as if theatre was a *terra nullius* to be populated exclusively by the latest trends and stage styles is a question that goes right to the heart of the profession's self-image (or lack of it). But, for now, let's just observe that while knowing where something comes from isn't the same as knowing what it is, it is certainly preferable to pig-ignorance and a handy way of gauging social context.

But why generalise about something called, in a coercively normalising way, 'Australian theatre' at all? Why risk peddling 'panoptic pseudo-cogencies', as F.R. Leavis once memorably described them? The answer is because every day crucial decisions, direct and indirect, are taken that affect the fate of the profession and, for good or ill, these are based on a general (i.e. national) understanding of its identity. They are mostly government decisions. Since the collapse of J.C. Williamsons in 1976, commercial theatre in Australia, outside major musicals, has shrunk to less than one third of the total performance pie.[1] The other two-thirds and more are taken up by subsidised drama, and the reality is that administrative decisions in Canberra or Sydney have a profound effect on the nature and operation of theatre overall. What matters is whether these decisions are informed or not.

The best use of scarce resources is one reason to treat seriously the notion of 'Australian theatre'. Another, more subtle, is the extent to which everything in theatre is part of a whole, and work at a local level relies on more distant forces, not only for infrastructure and financing, but for internal meaning also. As French director Michel Saint-Denis has written time and again, 'There is only one theatre'[2]—by which he means that, despite differences, divisions and diversity, underlying the production of any theatre worthy of the name is a set of cultural assumptions that extend across time and space to yoke individual efforts to a common frame. This frame is an idea *of* theatre that by necessity precedes any ideas practitioners have in it. And this shared idea is crucial—absolutely crucial, it cannot be stressed enough—to the health and hardiness of the particular enterprises that develop from it. While in the economic sphere 'being' may precede 'consciousness', in theatre props do not come before playwrights. You can create as far as you can think, and the parameters guiding your imagining are as integral, probably more so, than any system of external constraint.

And so to the nub of what's wrong with theatre today. It's not the artists, who are just as mixed; or the audiences, who are just as fickle; or even the money, which is just as tight (and as usual goes to the wrong people for the wrong reasons). It is the lack of intellectual grunt, of reflective power, that prevents the profession from knowing itself and applying the results in a practical way to different strands of theatre—strands that weave a complex, but coherent, collective web. It must be the purpose of any examination of that strange Platonic object 'Australian theatre' to get at the essential and informing ideas underlying the production of stage work on all levels and point out that if this conceptual water-table runs dry then the profession is in danger, almost literally, of losing its mind. The number of shows may be increasing—though, as we will see, the opposite is the case. The quality of those shows may be improving—though, given both the decrease in companies and in employment for individual artists, this seems doubtful. Official figures may radiate happiness and hope. But if individual shows do not connect up with underlying cultural forces, they won't last longer than their initial seasons. That's the reality. That's the reality that everyone working in Australian theatre has to acknowledge, however much they may want to lose themselves in just doing 'good' shows—the reality that nothing can take root in soil barren of intellectual intent.

1

Some figures: downsizing Australian theatre in the 1990s

It's possible to marshal an amount of qualified praise for Australian theatre in the last ten years. It's possible to skip over, sideline or deny the corrosion of its self-identity by either pointing out that many artists continue to do good work—true, but not the point—or by succumbing to the adjectival Blitzkrieg of cultural marketing that stretches belief about individual shows beyond the point of credibility. The truth is that the last decade has been a time of slow rot for the industry. Where good work has flourished, it has done so despite rather than because of broader social conditions. The lack of time, money, respect and care that are now constant features of staging theatre in this country debases the collective soul of the industry and grinds down the individual artist. There will always be a chorus of thin voices denying this reality, of course. Vested interest, lack of thought and, above all, fear cap an honest and open debate about the debility of Australian theatre.

Fact one: there are fewer shows on offer now than a decade ago. Invited by ABC radio in 2003 to contribute to a comparative discussion on theatre in Canada and Australia, I conducted a small but significant experiment. I examined the theatre listings in the *Age* newspaper, and counted the number of productions for the month of the interview, June 2003. There were 36. In June 1993, there were 56. On the eve of the interview itself (Friday, 27 June 2003) there were 11 shows listed; 12, if you count play readings; 15, if you include cabaret and circus. Compare these to the listings ten years previously (Friday, 25 June 1993). There were 34; 35, if you include play readings; 40, if you count children's shows. Even allowing for changing marketing strategies—the 1993 theatre listings contain shows which wouldn't bother, or couldn't afford, to advertise there in 2003—and for the fact that theatre waxes and wanes at random intervals throughout the year, this is nevertheless a jaw-dropping decrease.[3] In June 1993, the MTC was staging two shows, Playbox Theatre two shows and Anthill Theatre two shows. There were four commercial productions: *I.T.T.* ('the craziest talent game show the world has ever seen'), *The Secret Diary of Adrian Mole Aged 13¾, S.N.A.G.* and *Wog-a-Rama*. There were a number of fringe plays: Van Itallie's *America Hurrah!,* Louis Malle's *My Dinner with Andre,* Arthur Miller's *The Crucible,* Dorothy Hewett's *This Old Man Comes Rolling Home,* and a lunchtime show by the then-unknown Elizabeth Coleman, *Sometimes I Wish I Was Jana Wendt.* In June 2003, the MTC was staging one show, Playbox one show and Anthill had disappeared. Only one commercial show, *Scaramouche Jones,* was listed, a tour from the UK. And though fringe offerings were still lively—*Babel Towers* from Theatre @ Risk and Nicky Silver's *Raised in Captivity* by Red Stitch—their overall number was small. You can argue about whether such shrinkage is deliberate downsizing or natural attrition, a government-led cull of subsidised theatre, or a necessary cutback in the face of changing market forces. But you can't deny the marked drop in activity overall—a decrease bound to have a qualitative effect on the theatre that remains.

Snap-shot comparisons are borne out by records of the Australian Bureau of Statistics, which show a decline in the number of shows offered in the theatre sector in recent years, and in attendances. In 1991, for example, 3,453,000 people paid to see 16,122 performances of theatre work in Australia and (a small absolute number) Australian performances overseas.[4] For 1999–2000, the latest data-collection period, the figures were 2,792,600 and 11,988, respectively.[5] Since the mid-1980s there has been a marked reduction in the number of new productions offered at a state theatre level, with the creation of the Confederation of Australian State Theatres network (CAST) making it possible to share shows on a scale previously unachievable:

State theatre company productions: 1986, 1990,
1994–1998 & 1999–2003

1986	MTC + STC + QTC + STCSA = 51
	minus 2 buy-ins
	49 new productions that year
1990	MTC + STC + QTC + STCSA = 44
	minus 4 buy-ins
	40 new productions that year
1994–98 ·	MTC + STC + QTC + STCSA = 216
	minus 27 cast buy-ins & co-productions = 189
	minus 12 non-cast buy-ins & co-productions = 177
	35.4 new productions per year
1999–2003	MTC + STC + QTC + STCSA = 192
	minus 22.5 cast buy-ins & co-productions = 169.5
	minus 20.5 non-cast buy-ins & co-productions = 149
	29.8 new productions per year[6]

(Table reproduced by courtesy of Geoffrey Milne)[7]

Fact two: if fewer shows are being offered, there are also fewer companies offering them. In 1991, there were 197 year-round producing theatre companies in Australia, of which 129 were subsidised organisations. In 1999–2000, these figures were 103 and 67 respectively.[8] At first glance, a major reason for this appears to be the shift from an annual to a triennial grant system on the part of government agencies, a shift whose ostensible benefit— stability for companies in receipt of it—masked the reality of its implementation—the cutting loose of those who failed to attract it. With the introduction of triennial funding, the Australia Council slashed its on-going client base by over a quarter.[9] However, the historical forces which led to the reduction of the small-to-medium theatre sector—the 'alternative' companies—had been coming since the federal McLeay Enquiry first mooted the idea of a Major Organisations Board in 1986.[10] The introduction of so-called ceiling funding by the Australia Council the year before had shaken mainstream theatre. Poorly thought-through and poorly introduced, ceiling funding was eventually binned, but it put the top end of town on its mettle. Triennial funding, heavily over-audited though it may be, at least offers major companies some protection from the remorseless agenda-setting of the Council, whose ideological ferocity for the new initiative is typically in inverse proportion to the cash it has to support it.

In Melbourne, the cessation of Anthill in 1993—unique in its preference for neo-classical French drama and its willingness to hire artists from non-Anglo backgrounds— marked the psychological moment when subvention agencies ceased being interested in new companies and started chanting a 'maintain the infrastructure' mantra. Since the advent of triennial grants only one new Victorian company has attracted this kind of on-going federal funding (the Snuff Puppets). Instead, artists seeking support for new work have to battle for it on a production-by-production basis, hoping to attract a slice of an ever-diminishing funding pie. In the words of one director I know, the industry had 'swallowed the lie of project funding'—the Council's argument that fewer resources targeted at on-going costs would mean more going to actual artists. In fact, the result has been a double loss. Project funding has continued to fall, while an entire level of support has nevertheless been taken away.[11]

One area where the effect of Australian theatre's 'missing middle' can be acutely felt is the commissioning, development and production of new stage writing. Fact three: repertoire analysis shows that the number of plays by new writers programmed by Australia's non-commercial theatre companies has declined significantly over the last ten years. This has been accentuated by the fact that some present-day producers of Australian verbal drama have softened in their commitment to new work, truncating their seasons and/or programming more conservatively. As Geoffrey Milne has noted, focusing on the repertoire of 'alternative' theatre companies:

> If we look at the numbers of productions of new works—by known and new Australian writers and by new overseas writers—we find [... that,] in 1980, new works from whatever source totalled 47; in 1987 this had dropped to 35. In 1996, there were 37, but in 2000 the number of new works fell away to just thirty. We are thus producing one third less new work in this sector now that we were twenty years ago.[12]

To some extent the more frequent programming of established writers compensates for this. But it leaves the problem of developing new playwrights unaddressed. The present pool of established writers reflects names which first appeared ten, fifteen, even twenty years ago. Where are their successors? And where are the successors to these successors who should, by rights, be making their first appearance now?

In the past, play development was the task of companies such as Nimrod, Troupe Theatre, the Australian Performing Group (APG), Twelfth Night, Company B Belvoir, W.A. Theatre Company, Playbox and so on. In the last fifteen years a decline in the performing arts overall (smaller audiences) and of levels of public assistance (smaller grants) has impacted on this small-to-medium sector severely. In terms of stage writing it has had two effects. First, it has flooded mainstream companies with plays which, ten to fifteen years ago, would have gone to 'alternative' ones. Secondly, it has distanced the writer from his/her creative peers who would normally be the best people to stage their new play. The vast majority of currently established playwrights were developed in this fashion: by having their plays taken up by associates close in age and outlook and staged cheaply but imaginatively by smaller companies. When eventually these writers appeared in mainstream programs they brought both a playing style and an audience with them. Major theatre companies are therefore now in an awkward position. They must respond to an eroded, even demoralised body of writers, who nevertheless focus their expectations on these production programs. The danger is that, without appropriate opportunities, emerging writers will either not mature or quit the industry. Strong competition from film and television means that theatre is no longer necessarily the first port of call for those whose passion and ability lies in writing dialogue. The theatre industry can look unattractive by comparison: unglamorous, badly remunerated, difficult to penetrate.

From time to time, for reasons of absolute smallness of size and relative weakness of infrastructure, Australian drama has fallen into troughs of creative atrophy difficult to escape. The mid-1960s was such a period. After the success of *Summer of the Seventeenth Doll*, *The Shifting Heart*, *The Bastard Country* and *The One Day of the Year*, all four respective playwrights—Ray Lawler, Richard Beynon, Anthony Coburn and Alan Seymour—relocated overseas. With Sumner Locke Elliot in America and Patrick White lost to drama, Australian theatre was bereft of its major playwrights, increasingly reliant on overseas drama, increasingly incapable of imagining itself independently of foreign sensibilities. The rows which erupted at this time make sobering reading. They show the profession in disarray and disrepute, an anachronism beside art forms more willing and able to express a national voice. The 'new Australian play' (the NAP) was the focus of many of these rows. 'Why weren't Australian plays being programmed?', asked people like Leslie Rees and Frank Hardy. 'Because they weren't good enough' was usually the reply from people like Robert Quentin, Robin Lovejoy and John Sumner. But since 'good enough' meant 'like overseas drama', since the best writers were in exile, and since the existing theatre companies were leery of risks, then anxiety bred reality. Fewer NAPs programmed meant fewer NAPs written—which in turn meant fewer NAPs programmed.

Not until the 1970s was the cycle broken. For various reasons, new Australian drama suddenly became an important part of the repertoire. Older companies faced a choice, either to incorporate new plays—as the MTC did, attracting first Buzo then Williamson as writers-in-residence—or else to ignore all but the safest work—as the Old Tote did, another reason why it went bust in 1978. While many Australian plays staged at this time were not individually successful, the new drama as a whole better reflected tastes of new theatre-going audiences. This is the objective correlative of NAPs: new drama means new audiences. New Wave drama started small but grew stronger. By 1979, after productions of Buzo's *Coralie Lansdowne Says No* (1973), Romeril's *The Floating World* (1974), Alma De Groen's *Going Home* (1976), Williamson's *The Club* (1977) and Hewett's *The Man from Mukinupin* (1978), the movement was providing new industry benchmarks—redefining what 'good enough' meant.

While it is unlikely that Australian drama *per se* will again disappear from the repertoire of mainstream companies (it remains steady at roughly a third of plays programmed), nevertheless the danger of a static situation, which not only does not, but cannot, progress, is real. How the industry manages the problem of play development over coming years is crucial. Choices matter. The right choices, even if seemingly minor in themselves, can make the difference between a future flow of good new plays and a field bereft and rudderless, going nowhere.

2

What's it all mean? Qualitative analysis

Figures, though, tell us little of what we really need to know about Australian theatre. They give at best a positional snap-shot, a moment in time, frozen and extrapolated. The conclusions of the previous section are easy enough to rebut. Why should shrinkage indicate decay? Perhaps the industry is only 'right sizing'. Who's to say that 'Australian drama' is synonymous with 'plays by Australian writers'? Isn't a more inclusive definition appropriate in these culturally polymorphous times? Might not the disappearance of some smaller companies be the inevitable cost of the remainder achieving the next level of growth? Figures when used in the service of an art form at once ephemeral and elusive can be used to prove anything. They need to be contextualised and interpreted.

Offering personal insights into a composite entity like Australian theatre necessarily raises questions about the basis on which they are formulated. So let me follow the advice of historian Marc Bloc, who suggested his students assert their right to speak authoritatively by inserting explanations of 'how [they] can know what [they were] about to say?',[13] and lay out my qualifications—not too immodestly, I hope—for making the case that follows.

For almost seventeen years Australian theatre has been my most pressing daily concern. In 1990, after three years as an assistant director at Nimrod, the STC, the QTC and the Australian Opera, I founded by own small company—kickhouse theatre—which operated intermittently over the next decade in venues such as La Mama, Anthill, the Performance Space, Theatreworks, the Stables and the like. During this time, I was drawn into the development of contemporary verbal drama—an area which shapes my present concern with new play texts. At kickhouse we supported (but did not stage) younger playwrights like Luke Devenish, Pam Leversha, Hilary Bell and Sam Sejavka, as well as translating and adapting various foreign writers. Between 1994 and 1995 I was a critic for the *Melbourne Times,* a weekly metropolitan, and *Australasian Theatre,* an industry broadsheet. In 1993 I began my postgraduate career, researching federal performing arts policy from 1976 (the year of the Industries Assistance Commission's *Inquiry into the Performing Arts*) to the latest document making an appearance (*Creative Nation* in 1994). I next completed a PhD thesis on the Nimrod and, as my initial training had been as a social scientist (political economy) with an emphasis on statistics, I was able to correlate a quantitative breakdown of Nimrod's financial accounts with a qualitative repertoire analysis—a feat rarely accomplished in the world of arts auditing, where financial performance and artistic goals are treated independently, or hitched together in cursory fashion.

I then taught theatre at La Trobe and Newcastle Universities until in 2002 I was appointed Associate Director and Literary Adviser at the MTC, with a brief to develop new plays. Since then, I have directed four productions for the Company, all examples of new stage writing from overseas. I have published on arts policy, Australian post-war theatre history and site-specific work and been trenchantly critical of academic understanding (or rather the lack of it) of concrete theatre practice. I have researched the history of both the MTC and the Hunter Valley Theatre Company. I have been nominated for numerous directing awards, have sat on two boards (Melbourne Fringe and the Melbourne Workers Theatre) and worked as an usher, a stage-hand—and even an actor. In short, I have had extended contact with the four pillars of our contemporary theatre: practitioners, reviewers, scholars and policy-makers.

To get at its essence, the intellectual substructure of Australian theatre, it is necessary to look at the origins of the repertory system as they were laid down, in the English-speaking world, by its founders such as Annie Horniman at the Gaiety, Manchester, and Granville Barker at London's Royal Court a hundred years ago. The so-called 'theatre of ideas', vociferously advocated by the unsinkable G. B. Shaw, was the first and most articulate adumbration of a non-commercial drama, the cue and pivot for the sector which coalesced around it. The inspiration for the movement came from the notion of a public library. Exposure to a variety of great works in challenging productions, the founders reasoned, would educate audiences to an appropriate level of discernment, enabling them to take an active role in shaping the theatre culture around them. Through use of the subscription system, to ensure forward income, the non-commercial sector was born. And while continental Europe might remain the home of 'true repertory' and handsome state subsidy, an alternative had been found to the tired instruments of the commercial sector—the long run, the stock theatre and the touring company.

Transformed or reinvigorated these instruments can be seen today. The long-run show (mainly major musicals) is the rarest, but stock companies (the Bell Shakespeare Company) and touring companies (courtesy of international festivals) are common enough. However, the major mode of theatre production is repertory. Every major theatre company in Australia is an outcrop of the repertory idea with its four primary goals—the acquisition of appropriate theatre buildings, the establishment of egalitarian acting ensembles, the cultivation of locally-based playwrights, and the development of a 'discerning' audience.[14] These remain the super-objectives of all non-commercial theatre worthy of the label, *idées fixes* that constantly pop up on the radar of contemporary theatre—the MTC, still after the perfect building; the STC, finally achieving an acting ensemble; Playbox, eternally searching for the new edge of Australian stage writing; and various community- and event-based companies looking to pull that most elusive of creatures, the 'new audience'. Buildings, actors, writers and audiences. These are the amino acids that form the DNA coding of all Western-influenced repertory theatre in the last one hundred years.

My first contact with the repertory tradition came in the form that most directors make with it, as an assistant. No university course, however practically-oriented, can prepare you for the shock of stage production as it is actually undertaken by a repertory company. The custom of letting assistant directors observe rehearsals or participate in minor production-related tasks is as much inoculation as education. The limits of time, money and patience; the pressure to perform; the odiousness of competitive creativity that the system must perforce exploit; the variability of materials, human and textual— all make the world of repertory compromised, tough, occasionally desperate. It came as a shock to me, raised on high-minded notions of theatre-making and fed an unhealthy diet of semi-mystical manuals (of which Peter Brook's *The Empty Space* remains the bible). I learnt by watching the directors I worked for and whom I regarded as supremely talented: Richard Cottrell, Richard Wherrett, Jean-Pierre Mignon, Aubrey Mellor, Rodney Fisher. Talented they were, but it was the system behind them that gave their visions practical force and meaning. Only much later did I work this out for myself. As a director you can be loaded with gifts from the gods, but, unless they've blessed you with the ability to work within a given production schedule, a given budget and a given mind-set, little good will come of them.

Theoretically, this is supposed to be a bad thing. Theoretically, creativity is individual, radical, free. The rhetoric of change is mandatory for theatrical experiment. For centuries artists explained or excused their creations by fitting them into self-conscious models of continuity. But Modernism revolutionised the way art was marketed, as well as art itself. Since the nineteenth century, theatre artists have sought to portray their efforts as mould-breaking and innovative, even when, on closer inspection, the drama they have produced has been entirely conventional. 'Different' is what all theatre aims to be. And to question this, to ask 'why different, why not good?' is to draw uncomprehending, even hostile, looks. To the Modernist *mentalité* different *is* good, and the function of the good is to be different. In this way, the experimental dimension of contemporary theatre adopts a position of rhetorical superiority above other key values, such as audience appeal or truth to lived experience. In this way, too, the historical perspective which guarantees other professions a working grasp of their identity is excised from the minds of many practitioners.

Years later I was to have very different discussions with some of these directors, most especially Richard Wherrett, shortly before he died. At that time I was doing background research on Nimrod's three co-artistic directors—John Bell, Ken Horler and Wherrett himself—who were responsible for the company's remarkable growth spurt between 1974 and 1979. When the Old Tote went into liquidation in 1978, each of the three applied for the directorship of the new STC that replaced it. Why? What caused the three men to want to return to a system they had opposed so vigorously? And why did Wherrett get the job over Horler, or, more particularly, Bell? These questions raised other, structural issues. Perhaps Nimrod and the state theatre were not as different as they imagined, or maintained. Perhaps younger and older practitioners had more in common than they realised. Perhaps the notion of an 'alternative' theatre—the conceptual altar-piece of the New Wave—obscured values all forms of Australian theatre shared and that ran deeper than surface antagonisms suggested.

Richard Wherrett was appointed because he was the first of the Nimrod directors to see through the false opposition between mainstream and alternative theatre. In the year or so before the STC advertised for its first artistic director, Wherrett made several public statements that showed he was aware of the nature of the total theatre world in which Nimrod operated. With this insight would have come others—a sense of the partial, but nevertheless empowered, position of major companies; a willingness to shoulder responsibilities that came from leading one; the understanding that, to have theatrical impact, experiment and individuality must be offset by technical rigour and collective cohesion. And, underscoring all this, would have been a growing suspicion that Nimrod and the STC were variants on the same idea of theatre; that Nimrod was, in fact, a repertory company, albeit of a particular kind, and shared many of the burdens and preoccupations of its major industry rival.

There are many histories of the various waves of 'alternative' practice that have lapped the shores of post-war theatre. Few of them question the assumptions behind the construction of the category itself. As I began to do so in my research, I drew on my theatre experience to contextualise my thinking. I could *see* that actors, designers, composers and directors moved fluidly between different kinds of theatre. And, if not fluidly, then necessarily, because it was unlikely that any one type would provide them with the sole means of making a living. Further enforced diversity came from jobs in film and television drama—themselves subject to variations in approach, aesthetic and values. The rhetoric of the Performing Arts Board and the Community Cultural Development Unit at the time might sound a Cold War note, with mainstream theatre on one side of an impassable cultural divide, and the wild, mad and socially-conscious on the other. But the divide was one of resources, not root thinking, and what looked like uniform aesthetic blocs were breaking up (if they were ever solid) into diverse bundles of increasingly singular enterprises.

If there is no structural explanation for Australian theatre in the last fifty years being presented as an eschatological struggle between old and new, why has the imaging of the art form remained so trenchantly polarised? The answer lies in its demographics. Alternative theatre, as it expressed itself in Australia, but also in Europe and America, was a generational construct, a means of characterising the ideas of a particular age cohort of practitioners who felt they were fundamentally different from the older artists they first challenged, and then succeeded. As such, no absolute value should be attached to what is essentially a self-description, although it is profoundly interesting that young practitioners in the 1970s and 1980s should see themselves in such a stark, isolated and, above all, heroic light. It is not enough to say, in retrospect, that the New Wave was 'wrong' in its values and approach. What is needed is a comprehensive analysis of how the idea and the reality of 'a generation' took shape in the Australian theatre milieu. To do this means looking back (to the beginnings of government subsidy) and forward (to the present, to see trends established decades ago). From these thoughts, the idea of a close examination of both a discrete object of historical interest (the Nimrod company) and a wider pattern of cultural thinking (alternative theatre in Australia) took shape in my mind. In 2002, after nine years of research, my revised doctoral thesis, *See How It Runs: Nimrod and the New Wave,* was published—a perky, if limited, contribution to understanding the demotic origins and weird life-journey of Australian theatre.

The word 'generation' appears 82 times in my book, an average of once every three pages. The notion of a generation is exhaustively explored in the introduction and thereafter frequently applied to understand a period of profound growth for Australian theatre, the years 1973 to 1985. Two 'generations' of post-war practitioners are identified. One, coming out of World War II, I call the 'Anglo generation', because of the influence of the better British repertory theatres such as H. M. Tennent's Company of Four or Sir Barry Jackson's Birmingham Repertory Theatre. The other, appearing in the late 1960s, I call the New Wave, using the label applied at the time to the rush of new writers who, almost overnight it seemed, rose up to take by force of talent and imagination the commanding heights of Australian text-based drama. To someone used to thinking of theatre as a creature of funding priorities and media opinion, it was an amusing and amazing story to chronicle.

But in the dozen or so reviews of *See How It Runs* the term 'generation' is barely mentioned. Despite my best efforts, the book was regarded as having largely antiquarian value, a history of an over-and-done-with theatre company. Aware of how empty a term like 'generation' could be, I presented considerable primary evidence and detailed analysis to make my arguments harder to dismiss out of hand. But to no avail. 'It's really just a PhD', remarked the ABC broadcaster Jon Faine. Well, I couldn't argue with that (apart from the 'just'). What I did take issue with— again, to no avail—was the refusal to consider the book's central thesis: the generational fracture between older and younger practitioners as it existed in Australian theatre during the Whitlam years and beyond. The strained relations between these two age cohorts had profound consequences for the theatre of the time and ramifications for later work. As I followed the moves and counter-moves of internecine squabbling, I saw that intergenerational co-operation had broken down, and that this had wounded the heart of Australian theatre in some essential way, leaving great gaps and sad withdrawals where there should have been mutual understanding, sympathy and practical help.

Again, I caught glimpses of this sundering of relations, when serving as a young director, in the studied neglect of older Anglo artists—artists like director–designer Robin Lovejoy, who had a profound effect on my peers, particularly young designers, but was actively despised by New Wave practitioners; or John Tasker, the talented Novocastrian director, one-time collaborator of Patrick White and founder of the South Australian Theatre Company (as it was then called); or the remarkable Wal Cherry, ex-Artistic Director of the MTC and of the ill-fated Emerald Hill Theatre; and the many older actors who, with their memories of the Tiv, Phillip Street revues, left-wing plays at the New Theatre, and country-wide tours by the Australian Drama Theatre and the Australian Elizabethan Theatre Trust Players, seemed to exude body knowledge of a secret history wholly different from the theatre I saw around me. I began to suspect then what I now know, that Australian theatre is an art form in wilful ignorance of its own past, and the upshot is an industry that appears less interesting than in fact it is. The grey, official version can be found in any glib academic summation. But the truth is fabulous, intriguing, highly-coloured, a story of titanic struggles, colossal achievements, massive defeats, murderous betrayals. The onstage drama of Australian theatre is matched by the drama in the wings, by the ego-encrusted, soul-demanding slog to create an industry from nothing and see it prosper, despite everything, despite itself. But this struggle took an inward, self-destructive turn thanks to the lack of sympathy between Anglo and New Wave practitioners. The gap between them, which should have closed as the latter matured and the former exited the industry, caused a disruption in current practice from which it has yet to recover, and whose aftershocks, barely understood by those they affected most, still reverberate subcutaneously.

A number of key events in Australian theatre history were botched because of lack of intergenerational under-standing: the hounding of H. C. 'Nugget' Coombs, the best friend in high office that Australian theatre ever had, from his chairmanship of the newly-formed Australia Council in 1973, and the later ignominious relegation of his chosen successor, Dr Jean Battersby; the chaotic melodrama surrounding the collapse of the Old Tote in 1978, when an entire state company and all it represented—its program formula, its audience, its specialist depart-ments—were consigned to the rubbish-bin; the lack of succession planning in key New Wave companies—Nimrod, the APG, and Anthill—which saw them fail to integrate younger practitioners into leadership positions; and the block-headed ignorance of government reporting on the arts, of which the IAC Inquiry is the most spectacular of a number of examples. Underlying all this, the tedious daily friction between two different notions of theatre that failed to achieve mutual accommodation. On the one side lay the Anglo generation with their talk of craft, attention to detail and clear lines of command. Zoe Caldwell tells the story of arriving fifteen minutes late for her first rehearsal with the newly-formed Union Theatre Repertory Company in 1952. Director John Sumner made the entire company sit, in agonised silence, for a further fifteen minutes, to impress upon them all the importance of punctuality. Caldwell was never late again.[15] On the other side lay the New Wave mob—anarchic, loud, committed, boozed-up. Here was a practice bursting with enthusiasm and self-importance, clearly not interested in this sort of 'professionalism'. When Jane Street staged Bob Ellis and Michael Boddy's *The Legend of King O'Malley* (1970) or the Performance Syndicate its seminal production of *The Tempest* (1971), they flouted every rule about stage 'standards' as they were then understood. Their models could be found as much in the performative extravaganzas of the New Left, as in any form of theatrical practice—although the distinction, as with the US's Living Theatre, was sometimes non-existent.

The differences between the two generations of practitioners derived from two seminal historical events, which radicalised them in different ways. The Anglo generation were defined by World War II, a conflict in which trust in authority, belief in collective effort, organisational skills and never-flagging physical energy were laudable, necessary virtues. Opposition to the Vietnam War, by contrast, injected into the hearts of those it touched quite different values—scepticism towards authority, individualism, an organic approach to decision-making and an outspokenness—a moral courage—in the face of repressive forces. There's more to both types of practitioner than simply their war experiences, of course. But, clearly, the differences were profound. The abrasive dismissal with which they greeted each other's efforts did not flow from artistic vanity, but from a belief—held equally fiercely on each side—that they were *right* and the others *wrong*. As a result, lack of generational sympathy—the ability to see where the other was 'coming from'—quickly became entrenched. That's why 1970s Australian theatre has left behind such a pugnacious paper trail: inter-generational fighting is *everywhere*—at public meetings, in the media, across the art form boards, in and around the companies themselves (particularly the MTC and the Old Tote, as they dealt with inward incursions of younger artists).

The major damage this quarrelling caused was not at the level of practice. Disappointing though it may be that Anglo craft and New Wave commitment could not incorporate each other's virtues when they needed to most, nevertheless it is at a policy level that the fall-out has been felt most keenly. The rapid consolidation of the Australia Council's art form boards in the mid-1970s inaugurated a period of extended ill will and position-play. Jean Battersby, then Executive Officer, saw with alarm how the 'internal separation of the Council into art form sections, which had been an initial and somewhat hasty organisation expedient, quickly became the accepted structure'.[16] Limiting the composition of all boards to artists meant inevitably that broader—moderating—community views were excluded. The Australia Council's internal procedures became the target of prolonged public attack (in 1976 it was being investigated by no fewer than *six* official bodies[17]), but it had a decisive influence— how could it not?—on the way the government of the day supported the arts.

It is profoundly depressing to examine the policy ground

of Australian theatre from 1976 (the IAC Inquiry) to 1986 (the McLeay Report) and witness wilful stupidity in counter-productive action. Certain words acquired mantra status, and were energetically deployed for purposes of obfuscation and factional gain. 'Excellence', 'access' and 'equity' were uncoupled from their logical association and set against each other as if they could be understood as independent values and separately pursued. During the 1970s, 'excellence' became a key word for anti-New Wave critics—for example, Harry Kippax at the *Sydney Morning Herald* and Neil Jillett at the Melbourne *Herald*—as they savaged the work of new, young playwrights; against this, the IAC Report argued that the term was 'elitist' and that 'an informed, appreciative and critical audience manifesting their demands in an undistorted environment would seem likely to force on performing arts companies [...] a more important priority [...] namely, relevance to their require-ments'.[18] Donald Horne, appointed Chair of the Australia Council in 1984, tried to recuperate the value in his augural speech: 'Without talent you don't have new art. [...] There is no point in having community access programs if there is nothing to have access to. If people are against talent itself they should say so straight out, without bringing the word "elitist" into it.'[19] The following year, Tim Rowse, a supporter of the community theatre movement, came out against it:

> It is a fiction quite inappropriate to a pluralist society, in which culture and value are in dispute, to think that there is a single ladder of excellence along which all endeavours can be placed. [...] Perhaps [the term] should be eliminated from the vocabulary of public policy altogether and relegated to the vocabulary of private expressions of pleasure.[20]

So on and so down. It is the same with 'access' and 'equity', and other associated terms, 'relevance', 'innovation' or 'standards'. It is not that the words themselves are unimportant, nor that the arguments for and against them are not worth making (though Rowse's strike me as blatantly tendentious). The real problem is that the 'debate' is founded on such a fierce determination *not* to understand other points of view that any intellectual gain from the sparring of competing minds is lost. Tempers fray. Rhetoric gets firier, and yet more lacking in substance. Mistakes in conception are compounded by mistakes in execution. The introduction of ceiling funding in 1985, for example—an attempt to limit subsidy to mainstream theatre and redistribute the largesse to newer comp-anies—was not in itself a bad idea. But in arts policy, where how you do something is as important as what you do, the bloody-minded stupidity of Australia Council Board members, who introduced it without adequate discussion and no sense of appropriate time-lines, rendered it ineffective from the outset, and aggravated distrust between major and smaller theatre companies.

What effect has all this antipathy had on theatre today? It is a common conceit in both academic and media understandings of Australian theatre to imagine the 1990s as having ushered in a period of peaceful and culturally florescent co-existence. Below-the-belt stoushing over what kind of work might properly be called 'Australian' is replaced by a more pluralist understanding of theatrical practice. Strident nationalism gives way to concerned multiculturalism. As Veronica Kelly writes in *Our Australian Theatre in the 1990s*:

In its plural modes of address and its more concentrated political focus the theatre of the [1990s] evolved from the 1980s industrial pattern, which saw consolidation of the subsidised state companies with the commencement of concomitant devolution of disaffected groups and writers serving the specific energies of regional, women's, community, youth, gay, and lesbian, multicultural or Aboriginal theatre. Australian playwriting for all kinds of companies has demonstrably flourished extraordinarily in the past two decades, confirming that dramatic writing is now established within the broad spectrum of national cultural life. This playwriting is exciting and considerable in its range, displaying the survival into the late nineties of many authors from the New Wave [...] as well as the subsequent emergence of numerous important figures.[21]

'Even dung from a distance appears to shine', as the Chinese say. The Anglo/New Wave conflict over the defining values of Australian theatre was not resolved, it simply disappeared from view. Nor are those values adequately summed up by dubbing the whole period 'nationalist', a term that illuminates nothing and explains less. While current practice may be more varied in terms of its onstage aesthetic (but is this *really* true, and who can *really* say?); while it might be politically and socially more heterogeneous (although there are historical precedents for many 'leading edge' projects); and while the antagonism between competing theatrical approaches may not be so savage, nevertheless the great questions darkly raised by the immediate past have not been answered, nor has the hostile impetus behind them been overcome. If the guns are silent today, it's because the troops have temporarily run out of ammo, not because a truce has been negotiated. General exhaustion is mistaken for peaceful concord.

The legacy is an industry with the middle punched out of it. In every way, Australian theatre has fragmented and polarised. Mainstream companies (MPAOs) get bigger (the MTC's subscription base is at an all-time high; the STC has just taken receipt of a new 850-seat venue); fringe companies scratch about to make ends meet, surviving on goodwill and borrowed props. In between is a wasteland of non-endeavour. Flashy appearances at international festivals do not compensate for the grim reality faced by most non-mainstream triennially-funded theatre companies (TFTOs): dwindling programs, tight budgets and high audience expectations. It is as if even *the idea* of a theatre sector that might marry craft concerns with risk-based product is coming unstuck. Why do our capital cities struggle to support more than a tiny number of on-going smaller companies? The reason lies in history not marketing. We have lost the notion of a 'whole' Australian theatre, one in which each component part has a vital yet interdependent function. This has been the most serious casualty of Anglo/New Wave disaffection. We have lost a sense of over-arching identity in our theatre. And we need to get it back.

3

Melbourne Independent Theatre Project (MITP): Story of an absence

It is hard to provide historical evidence for things that did not happen. But here I want to do just that—examine a failed attempt at 'company consolidation' in the mid-1990s in which I was personally involved, one that sought to address Melbourne's lack of viable mid-range theatre. I then want to contextualise my account by looking at a major performing arts organisation, but one dependent in many respects on the health of the small-to-medium theatre sector around it: Playbox Theatre. This comparison, though contrived, provides a useful example of dysfunction in the industry that once was latent, but now is manifest.

MITP was a ghost project: conceived, researched, costed, that never saw light of day. It was a venture that sought to bring four small Melbourne theatre companies, each with a strong track record, under one marketing, administrative and production umbrella. The ultimate aim was to open a 200-seat theatre with a divided season, half the shows being drawn from outside hirers, half from the resident companies. The qualitative criteria governing the program were strict. The resident companies would be jointly responsible both for their own work and for selecting plays from outside. In others words, they had to act as creative producers. But not permanent ones. Each company would be on a four-year rotation as part of the resident group. In time, new companies would replace the founding ones— Chameleon Theatre, $5 Theatre, Hungry Ghost and my own, kickhouse theatre—while the shared organisational structure would remain.

In August 1995, MITP wrote to Michael Lee, Federal Minister for Communications and the Arts, raising a number of questions regarding the role and operation of small-to-medium theatre companies. This in itself was a remarkable event: such artists—by definition individualistic in their approach to the art form—cannot easily identify, let alone articulate, common ground. We pointed out a number of problems with official funding as they impacted on us, concluding with a bid for taking the sector as a whole more seriously:

> At a time when theatre in Australia is struggling to find reasons for existence, government priorities and funding priorities are neglecting a vital tool for a reconstructed profession. Taken as a whole, medium-sized companies have the necessary artistic past to contribute to a vital artistic future, but we aren't being given a chance. We aren't being given the opportunity of developing our work to its highest expression, of appealing to our younger contemporaries who are its natural audience, or of training our generation in the necessary skills that will ensure professionalism in their later careers. [...] The 'missing middle' from Melbourne's theatre requires a strategy for support that is responsive to its particular needs if it is to produce theatre of a high standard today, and seed the vital theatre of tomorrow.[22]

This got the ball rolling. In December the same year we were invited to meet with Haddon Storey, Victoria's Minister for the Arts. He was genuinely interested in our plans to 'consolidate' the four companies into a larger, but flexible, institutional structure and gave us $6000 to come up with a comprehensive business plan. Over the following months we devised policy in the key areas of play development and repertoire, technical and production, and marketing and audience development. It took *forever*. We were neither large companies with extensive administrative resources, nor individuals with money and time on our hands. We had to meet when we could, where we could, to thrash through a seemingly endless list of concerns and goals. But underpinning our collaboration was a belief—realistic, we felt—in an 'established non-mainstream theatre that [was] both artistically provocative and industrially viable'.[23]

We found a suitable theatre. On the edge of Melbourne's CBD was a vacant Defence Department property built just after World War I with plenty of office space and—remarkably—an indoor parade ground the ideal size for a small auditorium. The asking price in June 1996 was $1.4 million, at Commonwealth valuation. God knows how much it would be now. But given who we were, the asset was impossibly expensive and so the reasons for not purchasing it were, on the surface, fairly obvious.[24] It would have required extensive refitting. It lay outside the designated 'arts precinct' of Southbank and its environs. It was not a listed building Melbourne City Council had its eye on for renovation (unlike North Melbourne 'Arts House'—a venue of limited use for verbal drama). MITP faced further problems in a change of Arts Minister: in January 1996 Haddon Storey was replaced by the Premier himself, Jeff Kennett—and Kennett had no interest in small-to-medium anything, regardless of arguments for the strategic importance of the sector.

Thereafter came a year of hair-splitting bureaucratic discussion and lukewarm media support, as it fast became plain that the project was dead in the water. Still, the game had to be played out. Meetings followed meetings remorselessly. Regardless of the outcome of the MITP proposal, the arguments regarding the viability of the sector as a whole were not going to go away. So some ducking and weaving was called for. A pattern of official response started to suggest itself. First, deny that there's a problem (the sector is healthy). If this proves unsustainable, argue that the problem is naturally-occurring (the sector is troubled by definition). Next, assert that nothing can be done (appropriate intervention in the sector is impossible) or that time-lines present an insuperable barrier (it's too late to do anything anyway). Finally, if all this fails, change the personnel. Towards the middle of 1997—when meetings were becoming mercifully less frequent—fronting up to Arts Victoria meant talking to someone new each time, someone who didn't know the sector or the arguments and wondered—of course!—whether there was really a problem at all. I left a final Arts Victoria meeting with actor-director Aiden Fennessey in May 1997, brooding on the fact that two years' work had been for nought. But why had MITP's arguments fallen on deaf ears? Even if the building itself had been impractical, why had the challenge of better supporting smaller theatre not been more fully met? We didn't know. By way of signing off, I wrote to Arts Victoria and the Melbourne City Council to point out that the problems MITP had raised—that they had agreed we had raised—were destined to fester for years to come.[25]

In retrospect, it is easy to see why MITP drew no response. The time, money and attention were with the mainstream companies in the run-up to the Major Performing Arts ('Nugent') Inquiry, destined to begin its investigations the following year. The final Report was titled 'Securing the Future'. Given that neither the Committee nor anyone else seemed concerned with organisations outside the MPAO matrix, the inference was that smaller companies were not part of the future but part of the mix: a giant recruitment pool for mainstream theatre to pick clean of talent. This policy skew was buttressed by a new generational homogeneity. In 1988, the last of the Anglo state-theatre artistic directors stood down (Alan Edwards from the QTC, replaced by Aubrey Mellor). CAST was born, the co-operative mechanism by which state theatres agree rights and share productions. Throughout the 1990s, whatever top spots in the theatre industry were left to vie for fell to the able survivors of an ascendant generation. Now it appeared that the war *was* truly over—and the New Wave had won.

It seems gratuitous to add to the volumes already written on Australia's post-war generations. Yet, every time MITP stalled, there was a baby-boomer in a suit (occasionally a skirt), telling us why we couldn't have what we wanted, even though they were the products of the kind of assistance we were looking for. Most of the senior bureaucrats at Arts Victoria were baby-boomers (like its heads, Tim Jacobs and, later, Leslie Alway); so were their federal equivalents (Australia Council Chair, Hilary McPhee, and General Manager, Michael Lynch); and all four members of the Nugent Inquiry (Helen Nugent, Michael Chaney, David Gonski and Catherine Walter). And in 1996–97, so was every head of a state theatre company (Roger Hodgman at the MTC, Robyn Nevin at the QTC, Wayne Harrison at the STC, and Rodney Fisher at the STCSA). By the mid-1990s Australian theatre, in demographic terms, was a baby-boomer world.

The MITP proposal was incidental to that world. Most of our associated artistic personnel grew up in a very different social climate, with different expectations about theatre. In 1985, when I left university, I faced high unemployment, rising house prices, plummeting public services and political reaction from the New Right—very different prospects from those confronting graduates in the 1960s or 70s. The theatre I became associated with had to fight tooth and nail for resources, audiences and print-media coverage[26] and was not particularly concerned about the professional differences that obsessed Anglo and New Wave practitioners. We were struggling for our working lives, and there was little room for extended in-fighting.

All this seems obvious now. Today, on the brink of another demographic change in the leadership of Australian theatre—and of Australia in general—it is clear that the generational sensibility of which the New Wave was both expression and constituent part was a 'moment' in this country's cultural evolution, one that left its theatre immeasurably enriched, but with a swag of problems. One of which, I came to believe, was the obliviousness of so many of the New Wave to their own privileged position and the different circumstances of others. Did MITP face conscious resistance because it did not meet the accepted interests of our elders? Not as such. Did I personally deal with a New Waver who acted in bad faith to strengthen their own position at the expense of younger practitioners? Absolutely not. The New Wave individuals I met were invariably helpful and sympathetic. But they often struggled to see the value of work that did not have its predicates in the kind of theatre with which they were most familiar. Again and again I was asked to explain my position as an artist in terms which did not suit and in light of values with which I did not concur. There is no reason why the theatre practice of one generation should not run parallel to, and inform, the practice of another. But with the New Wave the choice was starker than this. Their demand was for compliance, not just understanding; loyalty, not just appreciation; conformity to their generation's 'structure of feeling', not exploration of one's own.

This is a subjective view, of course, but there is some evidence to support it. Let me briefly turn to Playbox Theatre, a Melbourne-based company whose operation overshadowed MITP's in many respects. Chart 1 shows the pattern of paid attendances at Playbox from 1998 to 2003. The information upon which it is based—individual and aggregate attendances—is provided in the Appendix.[27] Playbox is in many ways a unique organisation. Although classified as a major company, it has been devoted since 1993 to presenting premieres of new Australian plays. Mainstream theatres rarely make this level of commitment to new drama (no more than 30% of program typically). This is the province of the small-to-medium theatre sector (where new work of various kinds comprises 80%+ of repertoire).[28] But in the case of Playbox, its focus on verbal drama puts it at the epicentre of play development in Melbourne, and, since its accession to the well-appointed Malthouse venue in 1990, in Australia as a whole.

The picture isn't pretty. Paid attendances for the period 1998–2003 reveal a company struggling to attract patrons. Chart 1 shows a generally downward trend, but 1998 already represents a drop in ticket sales from the preceding year (28,291 down from 31,271). The average number of

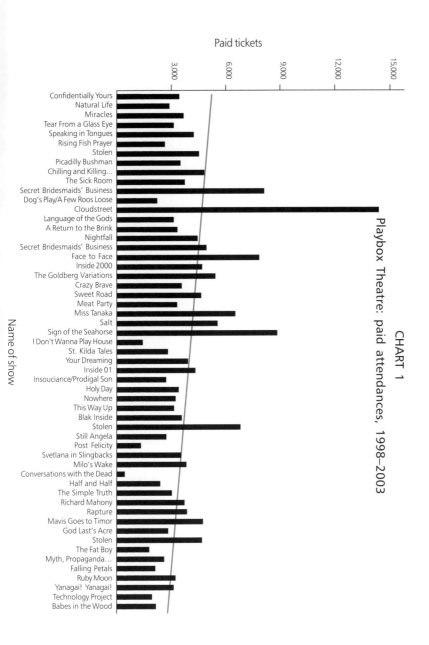

Paid tickets

Playbox Theatre: paid attendances, 1998–2003

CHART 1

Name of show

3,000 6,000 9,000 12,000 15,000

Confidentially Yours
Natural Life
Miracles
Tear From a Glass Eye
Speaking in Tongues
Rising Fish Prayer
Stolen
Picadilly Bushman
Chilling and Killing...
The Sick Room
Secret Bridesmaids' Business
Dog's Play/A Few Roos Loose
Cloudstreet
Language of the Gods
A Return to the Brink
Nightfall
Secret Bridesmaids' Business
Face to Face
Inside 2000
The Goldberg Variations
Crazy Brave
Sweet Road
Meat Party
Miss Tanaka
Salt
Sign of the Seahorse
I Don't Wanna Play House
St. Kilda Tales
Your Dreaming
Inside 01
Insouciance/Prodigal Son
Holy Day
Nowhere
This Way Up
Blak Inside
Stolen
Still Angela
Post Felicity
Svetlana in Slingbacks
Milo's Wake
Conversations with the Dead
Half and Half
The Simple Truth
Richard Mahony
Rapture
Mavis Goes to Timor
God Last's Acre
Stolen
The Fat Boy
Myth, Propaganda...
Falling Petals
Ruby Moon
Yanagai! Yanagai!
Technology Project
Babes in the Wood

tickets sold per show is a low 3,000–4,000, a figure that remains consistent regardless of venue, either the smaller, 198-seat Beckett Theatre or the larger, 490-seat Merlyn. (By way of comparison, the MTC expect houses of around 14,000 for productions in the Fairfax Theatre, a 376-seat venue, midway between the capacities of the Beckett and the Merlyn.) Few shows do better than the modal range, and some—*Cloudstreet* in 1999, for example—are presentations rather than in-house or co-productions, and cannot properly be called Playbox shows at all. Omit these and the trend in ticket sales is a flat line, showing that regardless of the seasonal number of performances—273 in 2001, as compared to 208 in 2000—the bottom line remains unchanged. Total ticket sales might increase, but the number sold per show falls within a relatively restricted range. The company has no luck increasing market penetration, and this is shown in Chart 2, a graph of the annual average number of tickets sold per performance—another downward-trending line.

In the search for detail, breaking down the repertoire into types of shows does not help much. New work is by definition hard to classify. Nevertheless, some trends are discernible. One is the declining number of plays by established playwrights, i.e. playwrights a patron (particularly a subscriber) might recognise and who might therefore influence the decision to purchase a ticket. Writers in this category would include Ray Lawler, Louis Nowra, David Williamson, Ron Elisha, John Romeril, Barry Dickins, Jack Hibberd, Michael Gow and Stephen Sewell, as well as a number particularly associated with Playbox, such as Hannie Rayson, Joanna Murray-Smith and Michael Gurr. Over time—and quite naturally—these playwrights are replaced by other, newer writers. But Chart

CHART 2

Playbox Theatre: annual average number of tickets sold per performance, 1998–2003

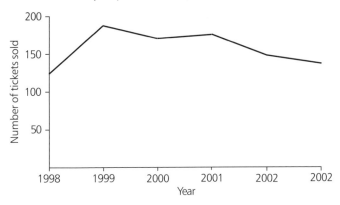

CHART 3

Playbox Theatre: paid attendances, established writers vs. new writers, 1998–2003

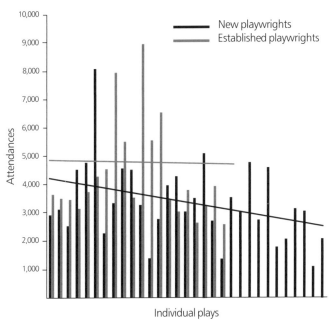

CHART 4

Playbox Theatre: subscription tickets sold annually,
1998–2003

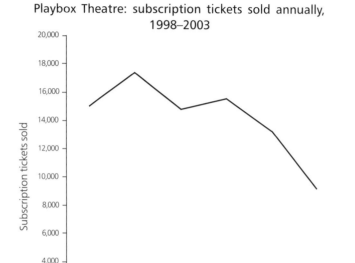

3 shows the handover to be less than successful, even relative to the overall decline in attendances, i.e. while the trend in attendances is downwards in the case of both older and newer writers, it is steeper where new ones are concerned. New work is doing less well at Playbox as time passes; but new work by new writers is doing worst of all. This inevitably takes its toll on subscription tickets and Chart 4 shows a dead-drop from a relatively high peak of 17,459 in 1999 to a period low in 2003 of only 9,118.

Finally, Chart 5 compares attendances in the two Malthouse venues. It must be of serious concern to Playbox that so few shows in the (albeit much larger) Merlyn manage to break the 50% barrier (the national average for

CHART 5

Playbox Theatre: overall attendances by venue, 1998–2003

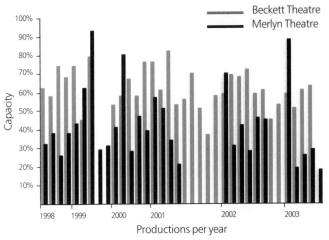

both small-to-medium theatres and major organisations is 60%+).[29] Four peaks on the Merlyn graph line are due to just two productions: *Cloudstreet*, a Company B Belvoir show, and *Stolen*, staged no fewer than three times in the period. Two observations can be made about this low strike rate. First, the company cannot find plays to reliably fill the Merlyn. Second, it is particularly unsuccessful at putting non-established writers into the venue. The ideals of Playbox's program and the reality of its playhouse appear to be at odds with one another. The evidence of 2002–2003 especially suggests that the company is being overwhelmed by its chosen task. Average attendances are below 4,000 in virtually every case—a revival of *Stolen* is one of few exceptions—and a number of individual shows perform spectacularly badly even by Playbox's low standards.

It is not my intention to put forward a comprehensive

analysis of Playbox's operation. The figures say nothing about its financial position, for example. Nor do they point to any single cause for declining attendances. No doubt intrinsic factors—management approach, play selection criteria, audience development strategy etc.— contributed to a marked deterioration. But maybe audiences simply could not stomach the uncompromising quality of new Australian plays, as the company itself intimated.[30] Then again, perhaps low attendances are to be expected when staging premieres. Playbox might be seen as an 'investment' company, responsible for developing, under adverse conditions, the talent that will be enjoyed elsewhere in future. The company probably argued along these lines in its submission to the Nugent Inquiry, who singled it out as one of four MPAOs to receive 'an artistic risk adjustment factor to the base level of funding', given that it was 'heavily committed to the development of new work, with an associated level of artistic and box-office risk'.[31]

Yet it is important to acknowledge the broader reality. Was it pure coincidence that MITP failed, and that the companies behind the project cease to exist, at the very moment Playbox struggled to introduce new writers into its program? Three MITP companies were focused on Australian verbal drama. In the case of five writers—Matt Cameron, Hannie Rayson, Andrew Bovell, Pam Leversha and Aiden Fennessey—there was direct confluence of interest between Playbox and the smaller theatres they were also writing for. And MITP represented only four Melbourne-based companies with whom Playbox might have looked to co-develop, or co-produce work during the period. Yet examples of local co-operation in their program are few, and those there were, either fraught with conflict (such as Ranters Theatre's *St Kilda Tales* in 2001) or belated (like Keene/Taylor Project's *Half and Half* in 2002). Only Playbox's relationship with Ilbijerri Theatre can be said to be both on-going and successful in attendance terms.

Staging new, untried plays is hard. Anyone who thinks otherwise is unfamiliar with the field. What is odd about Playbox's assay of the choppy seas of contemporary Australian drama is not the result, but the licence to do it in the first place. Because, as this essay has, I hope, made clear, developing new work has not traditionally been the province of mainstream companies. And while Playbox itself may have started as a small theatre with an eclectic brief, low cost-structure and the right to fail, rapid growth saw it transmogrify into a large one, with all that this implies: the need to serve its venues, maintain a subscription base and properly remunerate both its artists and support staff. Historically, few studio programs in major companies have had easy feeder relationships to their mainstage seasons. Think of the STC's briefly successful New Stages program. Or Theatre in the Raw, Playbox's own workshop program, a means by which it took an interest in promising writers. And yet in nearly a decade of operation only a tiny number of plays nurtured in this way made it into a main season.[32] The company's ambition to be a wholesale developer of new work—as opposed to one dedicated to staging the best of it—was wrong-headed, a misguided attempt to contain within the narrow parameters of Playbox alone the contours of a necessarily broader, industry-wide problem.

The burden of developing new work remains the lot of smaller theatres. Naturally, there is an overlap. Naturally, mainstream companies must do their bit to encourage writers and stage their plays. But to imagine that an MPAO could somehow *subsume* the delicate network of relationships that is non-mainstream theatre by becoming a sort of 'flagship' of new work betrays a profound misunderstanding of what a single company can achieve and of the historical trends which show, time and again, the opposite: that a resource balance between major and smaller companies is a prerequisite for the healthy development and the successful staging of new Australian drama.

Conclusion

Before concluding, I need to qualify some of my claims. Confiding in a colleague about my generally poor opinion of Australian theatre in the 1980s, she reminded me tersely that for some companies it was the best of times. She was right. The last twenty years, which have been a period of stupendous underachievement for verbal drama, have been lively and challenging for companies who devise work according to different parameters. The living edge of performance practice has for some time been with cross-art form, physical, visually-based or new circus theatre: Circus Oz, Not Yet Its Difficult, Legs on the Wall, Arena Theatre, Rock and Roll Circus, Back to Back Theatre, Strange Fruit, Urban Theatre Projects, the Snuff Puppets. The relative ease with which some of these companies tour internationally—no language barrier, low costs, niche-marketing appeal—has given them avenues of growth outside the domestic market. Next, my specific examples have been drawn from Melbourne, the city with which I am most familiar, and the template of my argument suits other states less well. Brisbane, for many years the Australian capital with the lowest rate of professional theatre production, has done rather better over the last ten years; Adelaide— losing Magpie and Red Shed and with a much-reduced state theatre on its hands—has fared worse; Sydney, with Company B Belvoir solid and a limping-but-still-alive Griffin Theatre, is at level pegging; and Perth's ability to foster theatrical talent (particularly writers) continues to be at odds with its capacity to do anything with it. Finally, I may have over-sold the idea of 'a generation' itself. Historical accounts tidy and tabulate, but the reality of any living seam of experience is that, however regular its structural features, it probably spends a good deal of time giving the lie to them.

Yet I think the big picture is broadly right. I have hitched together two phenomena—the rise of the New Wave generation and the decline of the small-to-medium theatre sector in Australia—and implied a causal link. That is, as the New Wave moved away from its historic identification with 'alternative' theatre, that sector declined, both in resource and rhetorical terms, and this disadvantaged not only successor generations but Australian theatre overall, by putting the squeeze on its most developmentally-minded artists. The effects are felt by everyone, but most particularly in the area of new stage writing: by playwrights, facing a widening chasm between fringe beginnings and the likelihood of future mainstream production; by directors, designers and actors, presented with fewer opportunities to grapple with the problems of staging local plays; and by audiences, deprived of the chance of seeing their own contemporary sensibility reflected in a verbally sophisticated body of drama. In this way, Australian theatre has done more than just decline: it has cut out its tongue.

Yet my point is not, in the end, to do with the absolute value of smaller companies or with the invidiousness of the New Wave mind-set. It is to do with vital connections that need to be made between estranged expressions of the repertory tradition, if our theatre is to prosper in any meaningful way. I have briefly described how this tradition played out in the unique soil of Australia; how it was transformed in the 1970s into a wholly distinctive mode of dramatic production; how intergenerational under-standing between different practitioners was lost; and how we are today heading for exactly the same kind of impasse. What I have been working towards is the idea of *wholeness*— that artists working in Australian theatre are connected by myriad invisible wires, and each of these sings with specific, but nevertheless, shared experience.

In this respect, it is to be regretted that the idea of 'the national' has had such bad press in recent cultural thinking. Perhaps in reaction to the strident nationalism of the 1960s and 1970s, some commentators have downplayed such notions for fear of fostering unwelcome chauvinism and xenophobia. A book like Tim Rowse's *Arguing the Arts,* which appeared in 1985, perfectly captures the aversion to all forms of national-imaging, replacing it instead with an aggressively pluralist take on cultural production. But there is nothing necessarily oppressive about the meaning or use of national terms. A theatre can be 'Australian' without seeking to subsume all differences into one monolithic, unaccommodating aesthetic. In fact, a sense of professional holism is vital to an environment of cultural diversity and aesthetic innovation. A genuinely multi-cultural theatre of the kind we all claim to want cannot be handed down by governments or community leaders. It is not a result but a process, and as such is, for the practitioners who have to make the art in question, a job of work. This job can be aided by a view of theatre production that takes into account the methods, experiences and values that artists hold in common, despite their racial, political and gender differences. Culture is shared experience and the impulse behind it communal and inclusive. It is neither a type of territory, nor a form of capital. These are at best provocative metaphors that alert us to its contestable nature. They blind us to the fact that creation is fluid, quirky, amorphous, providing in its themes and images the means of its own subversion. It shifts. Artists learn these shifts and how to work them. However marked their 'otherness', they address known and understood cultural codas the better to protrude their own specific view of the world.

To accept the notion of a 'whole' theatre is not just to give the nod to a plausible idea that deserves polite acceptance. It is to throw into reverse the intellectual tendencies of the past twenty years that have mistaken fragmentation for pluralism, and hidden behind the notion of cultural *différence* when they should have been trying harder to culturally connect. It is to see the distinct levels of Australian theatre as profoundly interdependent, and to accord each level the respect it deserves. It is not to paper over real divides, or smother argument where conflicts of interest exist. But it is to jettison the absurd and harmful notion that diverse types of theatrical practice have irreconcilable differences; that one kind is to be valued, the rest treated with contempt; that it is possible to benefit the part at the expense of the whole (the subtext of arts policy since 1976); and that individual artists are no more than expressions of their cultural origins and the theatre they create reductive and essentialised. It is to step back and embrace the big picture. Or at least accept that there is a big picture to examine.

As a director whose passion and skills lie in the area of new stage writing, I hope that a better balanced industry will lead to better opportunities for new writers and even—dare I say it?—better plays. In June 2004, David Williamson announced his retirement from playwriting. 'The story-teller to his tribe', as Keith Thomas famously dubbed him twenty-five years ago,[33] is leaving an industry that he once helped create. His replacements are not easy to identify. Over the last decade, there have been two or three new writers at most who have made it regularly into mainstream seasons. Australian drama has regressed to what the New Wave once rescued it from being, a cause. Like all causes, with each passing day of inactivity, practical know-how is replaced by egregious opinion. The hard yakka of developing and staging new drama is transformed into a specious gab-fest of wearying duration, the Search for the Perfect Play. I have turned grey listening to the prescriptive criteria a new play must fulfil to actually get staged. The Perfect Play must be funny and entertaining, but also moving and insightful. It must tell a good story, yet escape the tyranny of linear narrative. It must have memorable characters—but no more than six! It must have well-crafted dialogue, but not artificially so. It must appeal to everyone, and yet be confronting and challenging. It must be 'somehow' Australian, and yet 'as good as' overseas work. Above all, it must be new and different, while conforming to a formula that has proved itself successful in the past. In this way, the search for new Australian plays becomes a substitute for actually staging them.

While verbal drama would benefit from a more integrated view of the industry, there are indications that other discrete forms of practice may have reached the outer limit of their vibrancy, at least for now. Part of my job at the MTC is to keep abreast of theatre overseas, and accordingly I survey articles and reviews from Britain and the US, and occasionally from Germany, France, Italy and Northern and Eastern Europe. What I note with some astonishment is the breadth and ingenuity of art form collaboration that exists in many of these countries: text-based companies buddy up with physical theatre specialists; circus groups join forces with traditional playwrights; dancers seek out theatre directors; character actors vie to work with montage-style auteurs; new writing, adaptation, devised work and cross-art form productions bob around in one performance barrel with none of the territorial exclusivity and in-bred self-concern that marks different streams of theatre practice in Australia. Part of the reason for this liveliness is more fluid generational relations. When an older director like Max Stafford-Clark (director of the Royal Court in the 1980s) deliberately chooses to work with younger writers (Timberlake Wertenbaker, Mark Ravenhill, Stella Feehily), the force of the result is uncontestable (*The Break of Day, Shopping and Fucking, Duck*). Stage sensibilities are synthesised from complex and intriguing collaborative approaches. Expectations about what's possible are shaken up. Little of this nature happens in Australia. MPAOs and TFTOs, to bandy the acronyms, brand themselves as different kinds of theatre, focussed on different audiences, using different aesthetics. Better to collaborate with an overseas company, however unknown, expensive or politically suspect, than with each other. In this separation a world of possibility is lost.

In every way and at every level Australian theatre must look to promote forms of meaningful collaboration between practitioners of different ages and professional backgrounds. This might be seen as a broadening of the categories already deployed to judge the heterogeneity of the art form (adding age to those of family background and gender). Or it can be sold for what it is—a necessary alliance between experience and energy, knowledge and enthusiasm, historical achievement and future prospects. Given the way the industry has developed historically, part of this will entail a balancing of resources between mainstream and smaller theatre companies. The recent $10 million cash injection to support the latter is welcome, after the Nugent Inquiry's exclusive focus on the former.[34] Though weighed down by motherhood statements, the 2002 Cultural Ministers' *Report on the Small-to-Medium Performing Arts Sector* at least spells out the sector's overall value.[35] So does the 2004 Australia Council-commissioned *Analysis of the Triennially-Funded Theatre Organisations of the Theatre Board of the Australia Council*, a detailed look at smaller companies that tells you all you need to know about their fertile creativity, success in building audiences, and no-room-to-breathe cost structure.[36] Among major organisations there is some awareness of intergenerational issues. The current emphasis on succession planning is useful in the context, as are official mentoring programs. Some theatres—like the QTC—have elaborate induction programs which foster links between established practitioners and those coming into the industry for the first time. The 'emerging artists" money disbursed by the Nugent Inquiry to MPAOs, though it ran out in 2004, has had a progressive effect on other mainstream theatres (most especially the STC, whose Blueprints program is still the stand-out studio program among state companies).

But these are cosmetic changes. A whole mentality that has cleft Australian theatre asunder in the first place must be renovated. The profession needs to show itself mindful of its history. A test will come in a few years' time when the industry braces for another round in the 'funding wars'—and it will come as sure as judgement. Who will win pride of place in the egg-cup mind of arts policy formation in Australia? Mainstream theatres? Smaller theatres? Perhaps commercial theatre this time? There have been demands for subsidy in this area before. Or community theatre, as in the 1980s? Or even amateur theatre, the unmentionable relative in the attic, excluded from subsidy since its very inception? The grandstanding that surrounds arts funding goes beyond the dollars being vied for and reveals in glaring detail Australian theatre's self-image. And since the Elizabethan Theatre Trust opened its doors and its cheque book in 1954, this self-image has been ill-tempered, demanding and confused. No wonder 'Nugget' Coombs felt that his foray into the arts was the hardest thing he'd ever done. And has the art form that he advantaged so wonderfully ever shown *any* gratitude whatsoever? The best way of showing it now would be to take his vision of a co-operative arts community seriously. Any future injections of funds, however they come—*should* they come—need to flow across every level of the industry: there must be no implication that one sector is, by definition, morally, aesthetically and politically superior to the others.

While the burden of mindfulness rests on everyone in the profession, it will rest most heavily on that fraction of the New Wave who have survived in leadership positions. This will be another test. How will they see out their remaining years in the industry? By promoting the kind of drama which their youthful selves came to love for the benefit of spectators who, by and large, share their predilections? Or is there a way to foster another kind of drama that might feed the sensibilities of audiences yet to come? Playbox has shown one way not to do this. But are there approaches more likely to succeed? The challenge, for influential New Wavers in all areas, will be to get behind and actively support work that does not always conform to their definition of 'good' theatre. This is a reprise of the mêlée between Anglo and New Wave sensibilities that raged for most of the 1970s. But this time we have an opportunity to manage that struggle for the good of all, not just for the benefit of one party.

Better integration of different strata of performance practice and more harmonious management of different age-cohorts of artists—to put it blandly—will also contribute to the achievement of a third goal, a genuinely national strategy for Australian theatre. Over the last thirty years, the policies coming down from on high have, on the whole, improved both in tenor and substance. The Nugent Inquiry was at least supportive of the performing arts generally. No-one who has read the IAC or the McLeay Reports can doubt that beneath their 'rational' analysis is a strong dislike of the activity they are being asked to assess. 'Christ, these people *hate* theatre', I thought, as I pored over these documents. It's an attitude that surfaces just when you think it has gone forever, and it can be found across the political spectrum:

> One result of the public funding explosion over the past 25 years is that there is now a group of people who are predominantly under-employed, unemployed and in some cases unemployable. They believe that

they have the right to be subsidised by the working people of Australia and they have the necessary communication skills to complain long and loud if they don't get their way. They have found a sympathetic ear among the political, bureaucratic and cultural elites, including the media, and this has given them disproportionate political influence. [...] There is a mentality endemic in the arts community that if a company gets itself into financial difficulties then it must be because it is underfunded. The easiest thing in the world is to ask for an increased subsidy and to blame the government if an increase is not given.[37]

An example of faux-progressive, left-wing 'elite arts' bashing? Or bottom-line, right-wing, anti-subsidy tub-thumping? In truth, it could be either. The above grab expresses a timeless sentiment regarding Australian theatre, and points up the real difficulty the art form has faced since its inception as a non-commercial industry, that of cultural ownership. Most forms of non-commercial theatre extant have European high art (and thus colonial) origins. They prize the values evinced by high art traditions: formal complexity, intensity of effect, capacity for truth. The borders between high and popular art may be more permeable now, and thankfully so. Nevertheless, the theatre remains beholden to the former (though, God knows, it has embarrassed itself more than once by claiming its most experimental offerings as 'popular' works). The New Wave was an attempt to up-end this theatrical legacy and take aggressive ownership of it. In this sense, Australian theatre has never been an exercise in artistic autarchy, but was always culturally porous. It has suffered for its heritage by a muted and alienated position in Australian public life. Turning deep-set anti-cultural attitudes around is not just a matter of contesting opinions. Rational argument, as Polish philosopher Lesek Kolakowski observed, is an endless cornucopia. It is, again, a job of work in supplying, over time, the best stage experiences practitioners can muster to foster understanding of the art form amongst those who are dead set against it.

Yet it wouldn't hurt to sound united, to demonstrate that the art form for which we toil has a value and an existence that goes beyond gut feeling at any one moment in time. Donald Horne's complaint that the industry's idea of cultural debate is a one-line telegram signed by twenty artists points up the lack of articulated vision coming from theatre professionals on the ground today. At a recent public meeting on the future of Playbox, I was not the only one struck by the lack of specific knowledge about the company we had come to discuss.[38] And when, at the end, someone stood up—as someone always does—and said 'Who needs the past anyway?'—as someone always does—a vision arose before my eyes of a wheel of fire on which Australian theatre was to be endlessly wracked, our historical forgetting a constituent part of our on-going suffering.

To break the cycle of forgetting and despair will require that the profession make the effort to eschew divisions that once made sense but that now confuse. An art form raddled with rote sniping and low-grade axe-grinding must transform itself into an integrated, knowledgeable and flexible industry that is once again worthy of public trust. Part of the attitudinal change will be the emergence of a collective understanding of the past—about the real mistakes that have been made and the real damage that has been inflicted by thoughtless public policies and ineffective leadership. Another will be the construction of a vision for the art form's future. Like skilled professionals everywhere, theatre practitioners will need to articulate their individual positions while presenting a united front. The key word must be 'co-operation'. The different sectors of non-commercial theatre must knit together anew.

Perhaps it's true that Australian theatre receives a lower level of per capita subsidy compared to other OECD nations (though inter-country comparisons are fraught with difficulty). No doubt much of this money disappears in useless compliance costs designed to offset the anxiety of governments in giving it in the first place. And, yes, there should probably be some kind of 'artists' wage' that will allow dirt-poor unemployed practitioners to accept the social security payments they have honestly earned without having to re-train as arc welders. But the most important changes that face Australian theatre are internal, dispositional and inexpensive in dollar terms. There is much to be done if we are to get theatre back on track, but that work can only be accomplished with a collective understanding of the trade-offs involved in deep and persistent problems. So, for the final time: we must, as theatre artists, take responsibility for the present situation by fashioning a language of common cause that, while respecting differences, will allow the industry to present itself in a united way and not just as a snake pit of competing needs. We must re-discover the real meaning of the term 'Australian theatre', of which we are all necessarily a part.

Endnotes

1   In 1999–2000, Australian Bureau of Statistics figures show 67 subsidised theatres generating a total income of $71.4 million, as compared to the 35 non-subsidised companies generating just $18.9 million. See *Performing Arts Industries, 1999–2000*, ABS Catalogue No. 8697.0, Table 2.2: 'Income by Type of Organisation'.

2   Michel Saint-Denis, *Theatre: The Rediscovery of Style* (NY: Theatre Arts Books, 1963).

3   The AusState data base (www.AusStage.edu.au) allows cross-referencing of numbers of shows in both periods, but adds to the June 2003 total by (at most) four shows.

4   *Music and Performing Arts Australia, 1991*, ABS Catalogue No. 4116.0, Table 1: 'Number of Performances and Attendances by Location of the Performance by Government Subsidised and Other Organisations'.

5   *Performing Arts Industries, 1999–2000*, ABS Catalogue No. 8697.0, Table 2.7: 'Performances and Attendances'. I have chosen the least controversial figures here, given that comparisons across time using ABS data can present problems of definition. As a service industry of recent interest, the ABS has been reporting regularly on the area only since 1996. Currently, music is lumped in with theatre, and amateur theatre with professional, making difficult the extrapolation of some data relating to non-commercial, subsidised theatre. The figures quoted here, however, are relatively unequivocal.

6   Data from the last five years show a recovery from 2001 onwards and a return to previous levels of in-house production. Thus across the four companies we get: in 1999, 27.5 shows; in 2000, 25.5 shows; in 2001, 30.5 shows; in 2002, 30.5 shows; in 2003, 34.5 shows. This jump comes largely from a restriction in the number of buy-ins from the MTC and the STC.

7   See Geoffrey Milne, 'Hey Honey; We Shrunk the Repertoire', ADSA Conference paper (2000). Totals have been brought up to date by the author with figures from 1999 to 2003. The acronym QTC stands for the Queensland Theatre Company and STCSA for the State Theatre Company of South Australia, whose title has undergone more than one change since its foundation as the South Australian Theatre Company. In this essay STCSA will stand for the company in all its guises.

8   *Music and Performing Arts Australia, 1991,* ABS Catalogue No. 4116.0, Table 10: 'Number and Type of Music and Performing Arts Organisation by Home State of the Organisation' and *Performing Arts Industries, 1999–2000,* ABS Catalogue No. 8697.0, Table 2.2: 'Income by Type of Organisation'.

9   In 1997, 74 companies were in receipt of on-going support. By 1999, the number had fallen to about 55. At first glance, the drop is more severe, but structural changes in Australia Council funding meant that a number of youth arts companies were provided for out of non-program funds for a period of years until, inevitably, the need for a form of annual funding re-asserted itself in 2000–01 (information kindly supplied by the Australia Council).

10 *Patronage, Power and the Muse: Enquiry into Commonwealth Assistance to the Arts*, House of Representatives Standing Committee on Expenditure (1986).

11 Taking the relevant funding categories to be 'New Work'

and 'Development', and allowing for the fact that new categories regularly spring up and make a contribution to the support of one-off projects, nevertheless, there has been a decrease in the area in both absolute and real terms. Using figures from the Theatre Board Assessment Reports, we find: 2001—$1,514,062; 2002—$1,457,333 and 2003—$1,359,114. During the same period the CPI shows an 8.6% increase. Thus, project funding has decreased in the last three years by over 10%.

12 Geoffrey Milne, 'The Collapse? of Alternative Theatre in Australia', ADSA Conference paper (2001).

13 *The Historian's Craft.* (Manchester: Manchester University Press, 1954), p. 71.

14 For an early account of the 'repertory idea', see P. P. Howe, *The Repertory Theatre* (London: Martin Secker, 1910). For a more recent account, see G. Rowell and A. Jackson, *The Repertory Movement* (Cambridge: CUP, 1984).

15 Interview by author with Zoe Caldwell, 17 March 2003.

16 Jean Battersby, 'Looking to the Eighties—Trends in Arts Administration', in *Future Challenge*, ed. by P. Brokensha and S. Tonkin (Adelaide: South Australia Institute of Technology, 1981), p. 81.

17 These were the Senate Standing Committee on Education, Science and the Arts; the Parliamentary Accounts Committee; the Council-commissioned McKinsey review of its management and operations; the Industries Assistance Commission investigation of government funding for the performing arts; Henry Bland's Committee of Administrative Review; and a government back-bench committee, which arts journalist Denis O'Brien summarised for the *Bulletin* as 'formed to sop up the surplus energies created by the government's majority in parliament'.

18 Industries Assistance Commission, *Report on the Performing Arts* (Canberra: Australian Government Publishing Service, 1976), p. 20.

19 Donald Horne, 'Supporting the Arts in Australia', an inaugural address given on the occasion of Horne becoming Chair of the Australia Council (1984).

20 *Arguing the Arts* (Ringwood, Melbourne: Penguin, 1985), p. 34.

21 (Amsterdam-New York: Rodopi, 1998), p. 4.

22 Letter on behalf of MITP to the Hon. Michael Lee, 24 August, 1995 (document in author's possession).

23 'MITP Consolidation of Companies 1996: Artistic Policy Abridged' (document in author's possession).

24 By way of comparison, in 2003 the Victorian Government pledged $36 million to build a new 500-seat theatre for the MTC and a 1000-seat recital hall.

25 Letter from the author to Alison Fraser, Manager Arts Programs and Events, Arts Victoria, 11 June 1997 (document in author's possession).

26 The Australia Council's *Artburst!* 1992 carries selective information showing that during the 1980s reviews of theatre declined by 50% in the *Sydney Morning Herald* and by 200% in the *Australian*. The number of cultural periodicals available reached a peak of 51 in the mid-1980s, but by 1990 had slumped back to 24.

27 Figures kindly provided to the author by Playbox Theatre.

28 Cited in *Analysis of the Triennially-Funded Theatre Organisations of the Theatre Board of the Australia Council*, Australia Council document (December 2003), p. 17. This figure takes into account all manner of devised work. The percentage of actual new *plays* (i.e. play texts written by playwrights) is, of course, much lower.

29 Cited in *Analysis of the Triennially Funded Theatre Organisations etc.*, p. 8.

30 'Audiences Shun Hall of Mirrors', *Australian*, 6 October 2003.

31 *Securing the Future*, Major Performing Arts Inquiry Final Report (2000), p. x.

32 Between 1997 and 2004, 7 plays out of 103 developed were staged (figures kindly provided to the author by Playbox Theatre).

33 *Australian*, 25–26 August 1979.

34 See 'Mixed Reaction to Funding in Budget', *Australian Financial Review*, 13 May 2004.

35 *Report on the Small-to-Medium Performing Arts Sector*, Working Party of Cultural Ministers Council Standing Committee (March 2002); see www.dcita.gov.au/Article/ (accessed 15 October 2004).

36 *Analysis of the Triennially Funded Theatre Organisations of the Theatre Board of the Australia Council*, Australia Council publication (December 2003); see www.ozco.gov.au/ arts_resources/publications/theatre_triennial/files/ (accessed 16 October 2004).

37 Anthony Adair, 'Reforming Public Funding of the Arts', *Policy* (Winter 1999), p. 22.

38 'Storming the Malthouse!', meeting held at the Railway Hotel, Carlton, 17 March 2004.

APPENDIX
Paid attendances at
Playbox Theatre, 1998–2003

Name of show	Percentage capacity	Paid attendances
1998		
Confidentially Yours	62	3,494
Natural Life	32	2,960
Miracles	38	3,710
Tear From a Glass Eye	58	3,185
Speaking in Tongues	74	4,276
Rising Fish Prayer	26	2,674
Stolen	68	4,531
Picadilly Bushman	38	3,461
1999		
Chilling and Killing My Annabel Lee	74	4,810
The Sick Room	43	3,769
Secret Bridesmaids' Business	62	8,124
A Dog's Play/A Few Roos Loose		
in the Top Paddock	45	2,267
Cloudstreet	93	14,226
Language of the Gods	29	3,172
A Return to the Brink	31	3,361
Nightfall	79	4,478
2000		
Secret Bridesmaids' Business	41	4,988
Face to Face	80	7,886

Name of show	Percentage capacity	Paid attendances
Elegy*	53	1,054
So Wet/Like a Metaphor*	58	1,164
Baby X*	67	1,343
Violet Inc.*	58	1,164
The Goldberg Variations	76	5,481
Crazy Brave	28	3,603
Sweet Road	47	4,644
Meat Party	39	3,319

2001

Miss Tanaka	57	6,543
Salt	76	5,572
Sign of the Seahorse	68	8,866
I Don't Wanna Play House	61	1,441
St Kilda Tales	51	2,827
Your Dreaming	82	3,971
Ancient Enmity*	53	1,001
Seven Days/Knowledge*	56	1,071
Svetlana in Slingbacks*	70	1,338
Public Dancing/Bang!*	51	960
Insouciance/Prodigal Son	37	2,718
Holy Day	34	3,412
Nowhere	58	3,270
This Way Up	21	3,171

2002

Enuff*	59	671
Belonging/ I Don't Wanna Play House*	69	787
Crowfire/Casting Doubts*	68	772
Conversations with the Dead*	72	1,371
Stolen	70	6,880
Still Angela	31	2,763
Post Felicity	59	1,379
Svetlana in Slingbacks	61	3,540
Milo's Wake	42	3,858
Conversations with the Dead	45	446
Half and Half	28	2,431

Trapped by the Past

Name of show	Percentage capacity	Paid attendances
The Simple Truth	53	3,072
The Fortunes of Richard Mahony	46	3,740
Rapture	45	3,880
2003		
Mavis	64	4,792
God Last's Acre	59	2,807
Stolen	88	4,710
The Fat Boy	19	1,802
Myth, Propaganda & Disaster in Nazi Germany and Contemporary America	26	2,626
Falling Petals	51	2,125
Ruby Moon	61	3,239
Yanagai! Yanagai!	29	3,189
Technology Project	63	1,195
Babes in the Wood	18	2,160

	Total no. performances	Total paid attendances	Total subscription tickets
1997		31,271	
1998	229	28,291	14,836
1999	236	44,207	17,459
2000	208	34,646	14,682
2001	273	46,161	15,341
2002	243	35,590	13,199
2003	216	28,645	9,118

* indicates a show that was part of an 'Inside', studio season.

Readers' Forum

Benjamin Marks on *Survival of the Fittest*

I am in strong disagreement with Christopher Latham's essay, *Survival of the Fittest* and wish to comment on certain aspects of his economics. What follows should be received as it is intended, in the spirit of friendly, constructive criticism.

Latham claims that the 'market economy appear[s] to dominate every part of society' (p.8), but he fails to comprehend that the market economy is synonymous with voluntary exchange and relations. Surely, this is also exactly what society is. Then, on the same page, he says: '[T]he market does not care for us—it only cares for perpetual growth.' How can a collective concept 'care' or 'grow'? And, even allowing for the fallacy, why should the market favour perpetual growth? Growth of what? If growth of profits, then so what? How would the market get 'perpetual growth' without 'us'?

He demonstrates further ignorance of economics, when he says: 'It is vital we find balance.'(p. 8) Between the market and government. Between mutually beneficial, voluntary exchange and non-mutually beneficial, non-voluntary exchange. Between what people want and what government says they want. Later, Latham is 'fairly sure' that, if more Australians recognised the 2000 Olympic Games opening ceremony 'as a work of art made by fellow Australian artists, [then] ... they wouldn't resent paying taxes to support [artists]'(p. 48). The author's logic seems to run something like this: 'Australians are not smart enough to realise how good some of their artists are, therefore they need government

70

to forcibly take money off them (through taxation), because if only they were smarter, they would support the arts anyway.' If this is the case, then Australians should surely not be allowed to vote. If they are too stupid to know what is art and what is not art, then why should they have the power to vote for people that do? Using the same logic, Latham must surely oppose voting.

He goes on to state that '[u]nchecked greed is no solution [to the arts being profitable]'. (p.8) Why not? Clearly, he has not read Adam Smith, who put the facts nicely back in 1776: 'It is not from the benevolence of the butcher, or the brewer, or the baker that we expect our dinner, but from their regard of their own interest.'[1] Unless he assumes that nobody in their own self-interest would want to custom the arts—which I doubt. It would be like saying: 'Nobody likes the arts, so we need to steal from taxpayers to pay for it.'

According to Latham, 'Market forces will not civilise us. The market is no different from the jungle, except that the club is wielded more subtly. It is a struggle between the strong and the weak.' (p. 40) To compare the jungle and the market is misleading. In the jungle, *the stronger overcomes the weaker.* In business, *the stronger imparts strength to the weaker.* This utterly destroys the analogy.'[2] Also, '[t]o apply the principle of the 'survival of the fittest' to both the jungle and the market is to ignore the basic question: *Fitness for what?* The 'fit' in the jungle are those most adept at the exercise of brute force. The 'fit' on the market are those most adept in the service of society.'[3] 'In the market, the fittest are those most able to serve the consumers. In government, the fittest are either (1) those most able at wielding coercion or (2), if bureaucratic

---

[1] *An Inquiry into the Nature and Causes of the Wealth of Nations*, ed. by Edwin Cannan (N.Y.: Modern Library, 1937), p.14.
[2] Frédéric Bastiat, *Economic Sophisms*, trans. and ed. by Arthur Goddard (Irvington-on-Hudson, N.Y.: Foundation for Economic Education, 1996), p. 269.
[3] Murray N. Rothbard, *Man, Economy, and State with Power and Market* (Auburn, Ala.: Ludwig von Mises Institute, 2004), p. 1325.

officials, those best fitted to curry favour with the leading politicians or (3), if politicians, those most adroit at appeals to the voting public'.[4] If art is to be a legitimate enterprise, producers must rely wholly on custom, including donations, sponsors, box office or other sales income. If insufficient numbers of people value an art form for it to be profitable, then tough titties. What you certainly must never do is forcibly take money from anyone, even if they are silly and don't value art, as you think they should. You have no right to impose your values on others.

Benjamin Marks *is a hardcore Austro-paleo-libertarian theorist and activist.*

Clem Gorman on *Survival of the Fittest*

I am in complete agreement with the basic thrust of Chris Latham's essay. I have long argued—though not as lucidly as he does—for the arts to be controlled by artists, those coalface workers who make the art in the first place. Art is not comfort food, a means of distracting people from their troubles and their travails. It is an exploration, in which the artist leads his or her fellow citizen into realms of the imagination in the hope of discovering something new and meaningful about this life we all share. It is the most important activity humans can undertake.

Therefore, it can be argued, the artist is a leader, who needs to lead not only the art form in which s/he works, but also her/his fellow citizens toward a higher vision of the world. When they are led by people whose primary task is to scan spreadsheets, draw up contracts and schmooze politicians for funding, then the arts will start to fail in their central purpose.

Latham's emphasis upon involving the community, his assertion that Australia needs more outdoor art, his wish to involve the private sector more, and his wish to see art address

---

[4] Rothbard, p. 890.

topics Australians clearly love—sport, sex, money—are all 'spot-on'. Though his use of the twentieth-century Soviet term 'collective' may be dated, there is nothing wrong with his central idea that artists should join forces, help one another and collaborate. His naïve optimism is charming and, I hope, inspirational. On the other hand, he seems unaware that these solutions have been tried before, in the 1960s in US, the UK, and Australia. I myself was part of that effort. Actors' and artists' collectives already flourish in New York. We do not diminish ourselves by recognising what went before, by locating ourselves within a tradition. It does no harm to acknowledge the fact. And one generalisation at least might have been modified, the suggestion that ethnic blending will foster tolerance and innovation. Such sweeping remarks do not enhance the credibility of Latham's paper.

What's more, his suggestion that a recognisably *Australian* culture would result from the operations of innovative artists' collaborations goes against other evidence which suggests that in Australia all new culture, especially popular culture, is trans-national in nature. I simply cannot see how a small country like Australia can avoid the tidal wave of American culture, largely derived from and propelled by African-American culture. It seems likely that any culture created by artists working project-by-project in small, shifting groups would be overwhelmingly American in character. We are, as Latham rightly acknowledges, in a very early stage of creating our own culture.

One problem that Latham faces is that many artists may not *want* to cater to the tastes and interests of ordinary, suburban Australians. Artists are stubborn creatures—our choice of poverty has given us that privilege—and we tend to make art about what we damn well like, not about what we 'ought' to. He says that artists should speak with a single voice: but that's something I hope they never do.

Is Australia yet mature enough to engage with the idea of an *arts rainbow*, whereby a variety of messages from Left to Right (to use terms which in today's world are themselves increasingly dodgy) can be presented to the public: the cool ideas on the Right, the warm ideas on the Left? Can we imagine a school which this year stages a Rock Eisteddford musical satirising George W. Bush and next year one satirising the hypocrisy of a Chinese Communist government fostering capitalism?

What is missing from Chris Latham's vision is an umbrella organisation, itself run by artists, which could provide the technology needed by these ephemeral project groups, as well as the network of contacts from which to draw members of the groups, and of course the publicity system. Located at the Old Fitzroy Theatre, Woolloomooloo in Sydney, Parnassus' Den is an organisation which has its own ensemble of actors who stage rehearsed readings of new play and film scripts and which also operates as an agency. It is an ideal model for what Latham's vision needs.

Finally, may I suggest another model, which might inspire artists to take seriously the ideas Latham promotes? Years ago, the world professional tennis circuit was administered by an organisation called something like the International Lawn Tennis Federation. Professional tennis players such as John MacEnroe and Martina Navratilova felt that it was hidebound and not doing enough for the wellbeing of the players. So they refused to play any more tournaments—went on strike, in effect—and formed their own, new, player-controlled organisation, the Association of Tennis Professionals, which now smoothly and successfully runs world professional tennis. Anyone for … ?

Clem Gorman *worked as actor, director, stage manager and administrator in the theatre, before becoming the author of eleven plays. He is also the author of nine non-fiction books and has taught creative writing at several universities.*